Praise Quotes for:

HOLY AS THOU

Bittersweet Tales About Remembering to Love

"Connie's gentle sharing offers a sense of freedom and permission to remember how to feel. When one person opens her heart and shares her authentic truth, beautiful doorways open for others to engage and express themselves in love and safety. Each of our hearts holds this expansive power.

Thank you Connie, for walking bravely forward through your own doorways and letting us all participate in your passionate vulnerability."

> ~ Kerri Lake
> *Beyond Animal Communication*
> www.kerrilake.com

"Connie's pure and honest soul mirrors that of her equine advice-givers; Chasta and Gaela. Her stories portray exceptional "human vulnerability" and a rare alliance of maturity and innocence. Her straightforward approach to life will be appreciated beyond the horseworld."

> ~ Dianna L. McPhail
> Author of *On the Right Lead*
> www.mind-bodyintuition.com

"In Constance Funk's first book, *Beauty From Brokenness*, we were taken on the most delightful journey as she awakened to interspecies communication with her horse, Chasta. Connie's newest work, *Holy As Thou*, is more introspective, taking us into other areas and interests in her life. Never fear, though, as Chasta, Chad, Ritzy and Gaela continue to help Connie learn life's lessons from a horse's perspective. Communication, whether with friends or family, two or four legged, is the key to harmony and peace. Connie is a fine wordsmith and knows how to communicate...."

~ Sharon Roberts
www.horse-books-pony-stories.com

"A book will speak to you only when the author is willing to be perfectly Truthful. This is one of those books. Constance--you've done it again."

~ Patricia Kelley
Writer/Author
www.prisondogsbook.com

"Connie delivers a powerful message for those willing to open their hearts and cleanse their souls with horse wisdom. She prepares the path for us by sharing a wealth of references and openly guiding us through her own healing process. This book is the perfect companion to Connie's *Beauty From Brokenness*, evoking tears, laughter and comfort. As the last page is turned, one feels a tinge of sadness that this visit with a kindred spirit has come to an end, blended with the joy of renewed energy in living life fully!"

~ Jaye Nichols
Messenger

"Connie so eloquently leads us to the truth. We are not the masters of horses but must learn to love them as neighbors and treat them accordingly. Not to serve us but to guide and reflect our nature. Horses/animals bring us down to size as children do. Connie's wonderful stories invite her readers to reunite with the animal/right brain part of ourselves. Through her engaging stories, Connie Funk authentically and ever so gently ignites the reader to personal accountability, thus illuminating the depth of responsiblity in the owning of an animal and its domestication."

~ E. Bailey Tune, CST, LMT
Author of *Tuning In: Equine Cranio-Sacral Therapy and Emotional-Somato Release*

"Connie is a master storyteller, one whose messages are multilayered yet instantaneously recognized by not only the mind but also by the heart. I laughed, I cried, and most importantly, I learned much about myself and my relationships with family, friends and our animal companions/teachers. This is a must read for anyone interested in learning about the self through the eyes of another, in self empowerment, and in creating and maintaining strong bonds with loved ones. Read it and be forever changed for the better."

~Vicki Talbott, MA
Skagit Valley College Faculty Member
Psych-K Facilitator

"Connie has a delightful way of delving into the heart of her life's experiences, and exploring them as metaphors for learning and growth. Just as her mentor, the horse, reflects the truth of our inner selves, her stories act as a mirror in which we get to know ourselves and our world more deeply. "

~ Kim McElroy
Co-creator and Illustrator of the *Way of the Horse - Equine Archetypes for Self Discovery* by Linda Kohanov, and Author and Illustrator of *Way of the Horse Journal*

"Connie Funk is a master story teller. In relating her own stories with such honesty, humor, and grace, she connects us all in an unbroken circle of compassion, respect, and deepest understanding. This fine book will become your friend and bring you greater understanding of yourself and all others. Please give it to everyone you know!"

~ Rita Reynolds
Author of *Blessing the Bridge and Ask the Cow*

"A beautiful collection of stories told with warmth and generosity. Connie's ability to deal with setbacks and her unstinting search for truth and happiness is a lesson to us all. The willingness to admit her weaknesses and failures and to use these as a springboard for personal growth should be particularly instructive to male readers.

The strength, peace and connection that women derive from their relationship with horses is well documented and Connie provides ample evidence here too. My suspicion and indeed my personal experience is that men can derive just as much benefit from their equine partners if they will only allow themselves. When this happens on a large scale, we could well witness the sea change in human consciousness that so many seek. Thank you, Connie, for showing the way."

~ Mark Mottershead
Founder – HorseConscious
The new paradigm in horse human relationships
www.horseconscious.com

"Relating to Connie in so many ways, it doesn't surprise me that I thoroughly enjoyed reading her book *Holy as Thou*. Connie's stories so graciously invite you to see some of the pages in her life. I found myself laughing out loud to some and wiping tears to others. Her reflection of being a seven year old horse crazy girl completely resonates with me, as I too was that little girl, and am still her today. Connie truly inspires me and I thank her for sharing."

~ Lori Keehr

"It is inspiring and courageous when revealing one's inner secrets and truth be told I have always been terrified of horses. Oh, I have tried to become a horsewoman. I have fallen time and again and tried to get back in the saddle. I have lived vicariously through the experiences of my horse loving friends and family. I have made many excuses to stay far, far away from the majestic equine outstanding in their field. Not just because of their size and strength, perhaps it is because with their artful gaze they reveal all the fear within that I hide behind. Their simple neigh becomes my internal yes and I had not yet learned to embrace change and to live my life with an open heart...a change of heart comes slow... I believed what I perceived...and that while a horse may be a projection of people's dreams about themselves – I was not yet ready to accept their lessons. I used to think that the only change I liked were coins in my pocket!

"But with Connie's heartfelt revelations shared within the pages of her insightful book, I came to recognize that it was common horse "sense" I needed all along. Connie helps us to see that each of us possess the infinite patience, time, clarity, vision, determination and flexibility to connect with others, to take hold of the reins in our own lives and learn to fly. As Joni Mitchell so sweetly sang... " and the sun poured in like butterscotch and stuck to all my senses" so does the image of Connie and her beloved golden mare Chasta create a world in which we can see how important it is to discover our place in this vast herd of humanity and accept the bitter and the sweet. I thank Connie for leading us on the road to all those possibilities."

~ Vicki Mitchell

"*Holy As Thou* is full of thought-provoking themes from which we can all grow, such as the wonderful lesson Connie learned from her mother about never having a justifiable reason to be bored, "*in this remarkable world we live in where there is always something amazing to learn and experience...*" and the boundless benefits of "*communing with nature and the heightened sense of receptivity it creates...*" Her stories are so intricately woven with an abundance of profound philosophical messages, interspersed with such delightful light-hearted humor! I am in awe of how seemingly effortlessly she is able to draw words of wisdom from such an enormous variety of sources and apply quotes so appropriately to the messages. She is so generous with praise and appreciation for all who have touched her life and all that life itself has to offer! Her descriptions of how she overcame her fears support and validate those who have experienced fears of their own. Her positive outlook and the way she seems to ride the waves of life with grace and humility is admirable.

I recommend this book to anyone who seeks a deeper, more meaningful connection to life and all of creation."

~ Kathy Yaeger

"Connie is so caring, truthful and forthright--the light at the end of the tunnel for all those traveling on the path to illumination and connection, throught the wisdom of the horse. Blessings from Liz and the Herd."

~ Liz Mitten Ryan
Author, Artist and Animal Communicator

"Once again, through her insightful perspective, Connie has prompted her readers to look at life through a lens of gratitude, intense awareness, and compassion. Her writings are interwoven with humor, while from a deep soul-level, she shares some of her own experiences. Her respect for all of God's glorious creation is evident in her sensitivity to Nature's magnificent detail. Connie has once again stirred within me a renewed sense of awe and wonder, awakened my senses, and reminded me of the simple truths that I have always known. Her vision of universal truth and the interconnectedness of all life is artfully woven together with threads of wisdom, spirituality and grace. Her writings once again remind us all to be open and receptive to the still small voice within that is in perfect harmony with the Divine plan and purpose with which we are so thankfully endowed. By being open and receptive to the wonder all around her, Connie encourages her readers to reap the blessings which come from benevolence. She alerts us to the brotherhood of all creatures, and especially to our shared love and passion for the Divine Equine."

~Carolyn Allyn-Stone

"Constance Funk has created a heartwarming, passionate, and honest account of the many ways in which horses impact our lives. Reading Constance's newest book brings the life lessons learned from horses closer to home! Read and Enjoy!"

> ~ Leif Hallberg, M.A.
> Author of *Walking the Way of the Horse: Exploring the Power of the Horse-Human Relationship*, Founder of The Esperanza Center, and Assistant Professor at Carroll College's Human-Animal Bond Program.

"Connie's gift of sharing her 'bare-bones' honest life experiences have a way of inducing self-reflection in how one views their world. With an amazing ability to recall details with such a nostalic humility, you will either find yourself laughing or crying as her recollections and adventures with horses remind you of the miracles in everyday life if we choose to open our minds, hearts and souls to the wonderment of it all. Connie's stories are not only enchanting, they inspire and encourage people to love openly and honestly, finding the gateway to their own magical life."

> ~ Davina Andrée
> Graphic & Website Designer
> www.ArrowheadGraphics.com
> www.EarthWindAndHorses.com

"Connie's stories are like resonant threads that she has woven together into a rich and vibrant tapestry."

> ~Sandra Wallin, MA, RCC
> www.chironsway.com

HOLY AS THOU

Bittersweet Tales
About Remembering
to Love

CONSTANCE FUNK
Foreword by Stormy May

Front Cover Art:
By Deborah Koff-Chapin, creator of Touch Drawing™
All rights reserved. 2009 Touch Drawing™ and Soul Cards™
www.touchdrawing.com

Back Cover Art and Text Art:
Back Cover: *Halcyon*
Text: *Spirit Sketches*™ and *The Legend* by Kim Mc Elroy
All rights reserved. 2009
www.spiritofhorse.com

Graphic Design:
Davina Andrée
www.arrowheadgraphics.com

Publishing Works, Inc.
60 Winter Street
Exeter, New Hampshire 03833
603-778-9883
For Sales and Ordering Information:
1-800-738-6603
www.publishingworks.com

Library of Congress Number: 2009903778
ISBN 13: 978-1-933002-37-8
ISBN 10: 1-933002-37-9

Printed in Canada.

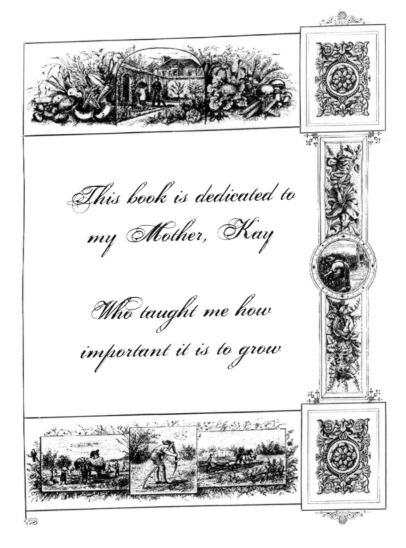

This book is dedicated to
my Mother, Kay

Who taught me how
important it is to grow

Table of Contents:

Foreword

It seems predestined that Connie would find me before I had even finished editing *The Path of the Horse*. Even though physically there were hundreds of miles between us, her life operates under different laws, and the law that brings together two women who have an interest in understanding the mysteries of horses and life was operating at full force. Connie sent a message and it appeared in my email inbox telling me how eager she was to see this documentary that I was still 9 months away from releasing. She excitedly told me that she was writing a book called *Beauty from Brokenness* about the education she was receiving from her horse Chasta.

I read the manuscript for *Beauty from Brokenness* as I finished editing my own project and

1

was particularly struck by Connie's ability to see the lessons presented to her, whether it was through interactions with her horses, family, or whatever else offered itself in her richly lived life. I have known very few people who jump from one opportunity to the next with such apparent facility, and then answer the call to write about it in an honest, open-hearted way in order to share their journey with others.

Connie and I were recently reminiscing about one of our favorite authors, James Herriot. As we talked about his *All Creatures Great and Small* series, it struck me that this book, *Holy as Thou* has been written from the same place. Connie has the same gift that made James Herriot such a beloved author, the gift of being able to see the miracles in such every day occurrences as the birth of baby ducks and the challenges of owning a horse who always seems to be one step ahead of her.

In the same way Connie and I were drawn together, this book has now found you, the reader, and I urge you to let that magic pull you towards the next step of your own journey. It might be a reference she shares, a story she tells, or even a picture or a quote that you see in the following pages that is exactly what you were looking for.

I want to send you into this book with a quote that you will understand better as you read through the following pages. It was first spoken by a woman who gave us a shining example of what a life can look like when it is lived in service to something larger than oneself; but for now, let's start with the words and when you get to know Connie better, she'll tell you who said it.

"We cannot do great things,
only small things with great love."

May you recognize this book as a small thing, done with great love.

~ Stormy May, Producer
The Path of the Horse Documentary

Introduction

In the life of each mortal soul, there are defining moments. Events that stand out uniquely and shape the formation of the individual. Some of these moments may be intensely sorrowful of even filled with terror. Others are times of incredible joy or the fulfilling pride of a great sense of accomplishment---a dream realized. And perhaps the grandest moments in time truly stop the clock and are utterly timeless, when we feel known, understood, seen and heard. Connected to all life in the quiet breath of a sunset, looking down to see the contented smile of a baby at our breast, the seamless movement of ducks on a pond. These simple moments define us since they help us to understand our place in the universe.

Some examples in my own life would be in the autumn of my seventh year as I watched my parents and my favorite adult neighbors sit closely together on the lumpy brown sofa in the family room of our suburban rambler house clutching each other and sobbing as they watched the funeral procession of then President John Fitzgerald Kennedy on our nineteen inch black and white television. How their sobs and wails reached a crescendo as John Jr., wearing a long coat and short pants, saluted the casket while the haunting sound of the clip clop of the hooves of the riderless horse, Black Jack, echoed in the distance and the polished high boots turned backwards in the stirrups of the empty saddle reflected the sunlight.

I had no memory of these four adults, joined together in tragedy by the proximity of being next door neighbors, ever crying prior to this day. Certainly not wailing. And these familiar faces, etched with pain and what felt like intense fear to my little self with the pixie haircut, standing behind them, caused me to be uncharacteristically mute with my own confusion.

Usually these neighbors brought joy and laughter into our lives. Beautiful brown-eyed Elaine always tucked her plump, chewy molasses cookies into my lunchbox whenever I snuck over there to have her tie the bow in the back of my dress before school, knowing that her kitchen would have that familiar and comforting gingery smell and that there would be a smile and a warm hug from her before sending me on my way. And her husband, Lew? Towering over all of us, he had a deep baritone voice and a hearty laugh to match Elaine's easy giggles, and was the biggest kid in both families. I mean, he drove a *candy* truck for a living that was parked outside their house with larger than life pictures of the sugary concoctions painted on the sides. He might as well have been Willy Wonka. So they always had a dish of those licorice assortments with the stacks of pink and yellow coconut layers within our reach.

A few months before the tragedy in Dallas that stunned our nation, Lew and Elaine had stored the bicycle that was to be my surprise birthday gift in their garage. When it came time to unveil it, and I was to eagerly take my maiden voyage, this rascal of a man ran in front of me and jumped aboard and took off up the street ringing the bell again and again for all to hear, a wild gleam in his usually twinkling eyes. Only because it was *him* did I not fall apart when my new pink and white bike temporarily slipped from my grasp.

And, of course, the celebratory joy of our son Evan's entrance into our lives and the indescribable awe of not only witnessing the miracle of his birth, but being completely re-born by fully engaging in it. Hearing *"It's a boy!"* from our physician as I watched him emerge from *my* womb to *his* world, red and swollen but incredibly serene, knowing from deep within that with his birth, my husband, Gary, and I were given this gift of being born anew. Gary's projectile tears of joy landed all over Evan and everyone in the vicinity as he thrust his son close to the witnesses, repeating over and over in a soft, incredulous tone, "He's a *miracle!*"

And what has become known in shorthand in our culture as 9-11. On that fateful day as I was about to leave to take Evan to middle school in his new fall clothes, hearing Gary's tense voice on the phone, almost a shout, urgently telling me to stay home until he could join us and that New York was under siege. He told us to turn on the television, which, a generation later was a wide screen in color with a remote that required me to have Evan find the national news program. Gary had already left for work when he heard the broadcast and had turned around. Shortly after the phone call, he burst in the door with a look of gravity and confusion on his face and swept Evan and me into his arms. We stood in front of the television and watched the images that would be forever etched into our minds and the collective consciousness: a jet plane crashing into the Twin Towers in New York City. Evan looked at us searchingly, his eleven year old eyes wild with fright and asked, "Is it a *war*?!" In that moment, we realized many families had been torn apart and the world forever changed.

And then, in the autumn of my forty seventh year, I received a gifthorse, literally, from Gary and Evan. She looked like the horse of my dreams when I saw her in the distance by moonlight the night I returned from a trip to France with my parents and my brother. It was the first time I had ever really been separated from my husband and son for any length of time, and it was September 11, a year later, so my family (and the rest of the world) was still feeling vulnerable.

On the day I was riding a dark bay horse across the ocean halfway around the planet with a handsome black haired young man named Damien, our host from his country bed and breakfast guest house in the Provence area of southern France, my husband and son had collaborated to purchase a Palomino colored mare from a handsome young black haired man named Damien close to our home for my birthday gift…...

Then they had left for a school field trip to a mountain camp on the day I was scheduled to return and left me a note wishing me a "Happy Birthday" and announcing the arrival of my gift, a horse named Chasta.

In the state of arousal and exhaustion that international travel creates, I plucked a round, red apple from our orchard that was in a bowl on the kitchen table, and taking a juicy bite of it, headed out in the middle of the night to meet her. Our three dogs had all been greeting me enthusiastically and were over the top in their barking, jumping and licking, all vying for my attention. I thought they were just happy to see me, but missed their most urgent message: "There's a *horse* out there!"

When I finally saw her silhouette in the backdrop of the moonlight, I approached and could sense how tentative she was. Or was that *me?* I believe it was mutual. Calling her name caused her to turn and look over at me warily. Offering her the apple in my outstretched hand, we walked toward each other until I could see a lightening-shaped scar down her face and in that moment I felt a sharp visceral wrenching in my gut while my eyes saw sparks fly off the length of it. It was a mystical, eerie moment and I felt a palpable boundary emerge that stopped me in my tracks. She finally stretched her nose out and plucked the apple from my palm and retreated into the darkness.

Waking up the next morning, it felt odd to be in my own bed with familiar surroundings as I remembered my dream of riding a golden horse in the French countryside---my day and night dreams had overlapped. Seeing Chasta in the morning after our strange first encounter, I had a clear message from the Heavens that she had come into my life to change it forever.

First, she scared me to death. Taking me on a wild ride that terrified us both, crashing through the woods, off the trail, flying over everything in our path, she ignited the eruption of the volcano within me that had been boiling beneath the surface for years. When the rocketship finally landed and I realized that we had survived, our combined six legs, shaking with near paralyzing fear, took us home, on the ground.

That night in bed, as the adrenaline in my system started to wane, I realized that Chas-

ta had jump started my heart, equine elec-
troshock therapy style. She had scared me
back to life. I wanted to live — really *LIVE! To
become fully alive in a new way.* A teacher, this
sentient being would take me on a soul journey like no other. Ready or not.

In the darkness, I heard Gary's weary voice,
"I am sorry that I got you the wrong horse."
And what I heard was "I am sorry that I am
the wrong husband." How much of the time
in our roller coaster marriage had I given
him that impression without saying it in so
many words? At that time, after twenty five
years of marriage that had survived the pain
of addictions, death, betrayals, financial
pressures, and illness, it was time to learn to
really *thrive*, not merely hang on with the te-
nacity of two bulldogs playing tug of war.

Chasta had arrived to become my midlife
coach and accountability partner. My personal growth mentor. And my spiritual advisor, for above that scar running down her
long face, I saw the tender eyes of God looking back at me through hers in a way that
told me this awakening was my gift to receive.

My experiences with Chasta have been so
powerful and life changing and have affect-

ed my perspective so much that I felt compelled to share them. I have always been a storyteller. As a child, I was the one amongst others who was the spokesperson: for the scavenger hunt, to get permission from the parents, (mine or otherwise), to play the lead in the class play in elementary school. Many times over the years, others have told me that I should pen my stories. One special friend suggested that she had enough material to publish a book from the letters that I had sent to her.

When I made the decision to record my experiences, they literally poured out of me. First, the bones downloaded as fast as I could put pen to paper and in the weeks and months ahead it fleshed out and took form that felt like I had been given this work as a sacred assignment. That I have been appointed as a scribe for the human-animal-nature consciousness that is expanding and offering to save humanity from itself.

Those stories became my first book---**Beauty From Brokenness** *Bits and Pieces of my Journey Into Wholeness.* The experience was a gateway for me to share *more* defining moments of my life in this volume in the hopes that some of the lessons I am learning will touch your heart and soul in ways that remind us we are all One With God.

For a horse crazy seven-year-old who got a bicycle with a bell instead of the pony of her dreams, Chasta had come forty years later to lead me home to myself.

Peace be with You!

Constance Funk
Woodylane Farm

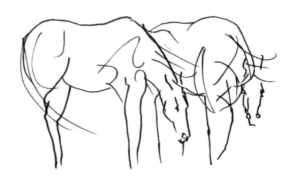

PART I

Golden Days
With a Chance
of Precipitation

Chapter One

Holy As Thou

A good book is a gift. It has the ability to inform, entertain, instruct, inspire and transform. And the best ones have room on the pages for the reader to feel seen and heard and to have his or her story connect so that the sum total of the author's words and the reader's feelings create a new conversation. And everyone knows to avoid starting a conversation about political or spiritual subjects, especially in the beginning! And yet, we live in a time on this precious planet where I feel it is so important to get to the heart of the matter. And to the extent that is possible, to live our lives from that place. So I will take a leap of faith and share my heart with you.

Since I have been a tiny child, I felt from an inner knowing that God is the holy of holies. Yet for all of creation, I do not believe there is a hierarchy for holiness. Certainly I will acknowledge a Bell curve for the quality of personal choice making and behavior, but not the *inherent holiness,* the inner sacred perfection that is our very *being.* Our birthright. We are *all* chosen to be given the gift of the Holy Spirit. We may not be aware of it on a conscious level or feel guided by it, yet it animates our every cell.

When the assembly gathered to create the Declaration of Independence to proclaim the early colonies as The United States of America in the year 1776, they wrote the words: *All men are created equal.* A wise and truthful statement, although not their own. "All men are created equal" is the design and proclamation of God. All men, of course, includes the mothers who bore them in their wombs and raised them to be men of character and integrity. On that historic day many of them had wives and young sons and daughters destined to become the fabric of the next generation.

I, (and therefore my son) am a relative of Josiah Bartlett from New Hampshire, who signed his name directly after John Hancock, famous for scribing his own especially large and bold so that it would be seen and remembered. As my thoughts wander in meditation about the energy and intention of the dream in that room many years ago, they slowly swirl and crystallize until I feel a profound sense of peace and gratitude for the nobility of those humble men gathered to have the courage to lead from their hearts with those prophetic words.

We *are all created equal* in the eyes of God. It is not based on race, creed, color, faith tradition or character but on the gift of love that is bestowed upon the conception of every new life. And that includes all life in the plant and animal kingdoms. Each life form is a student as well as teacher. If, indeed, mankind has a unique role in all of creation, it was intended as a co-operative partnership. To date, as a species the model humans have used is largely one of arrogance and domination and competitiveness, and frankly to a huge extent, we have botched the job terribly, polluting the planet, driving vital species to extinction that we were designed to be interdependent with. The new paradigm *must* be one of partnership, stewardship and co-operation with a sense of all embracing wholism if we are to survive. And we were designed to *thrive*, not merely survive, living in fear and chaos. So this is a very unique and exciting and hopeful time in history, where we can create sustainable systems of cooperative governments, faith traditions and international economies. Where the abundance and beauty of the universe is shared, respected and preserved. To work and play along side each other, combining the gifts of technology with the natural rhythms of the planet. Intellect and instinct, hand in hand.

With *complete and due* respect to all of the sages and saints throughout the ages of every faith tradition when they are described as holy men and women, I believe it is due to their recognition and complete awareness of their personal connection to God and all of creation. Their unique and peaceful commitments to mankind and our planet is exemplary and magnificent so these souls make it easy for me to identify their holiness shining through. Yet their holiness should, in my opinion, not be measured by their deeds but by their inner perfection and we can all be inspired by that in them which also dwells in us. And the deeds, the good work, is the *fruit* of the holiness which animates them. And that example can shine for everyone in recognition that we can *all* be saints in progress.

But what of the young man who becomes a meth addict who sells the drug to support his habit? If I forget, (as I far too often do) even for a moment, of his sacred infrastructure, his inherent holiness, than all too easily I can judge him as broken beyond repair rather than in need of my recognition that he is my brother. How can I make a difference when there is so much injustice, such an imbalance of what appears to be power? There are no easy answers, I realize, yet I feel like the Pollyanna character gets such a bad rap as a simple, uninformed person with idealized notions, yet her choice is to focus on the good in all, and by doing so, the good enlarges, hearts heal and there is love, forgiveness and connection. *Why is that considered so naïve?* She is a model for positive thinking and our thoughts have the power to create reality. When one young person, Pollyanna, is able to see the inner light of others, regardless of their own blindness to it, and warm the hearts of an entire community to become reconciled, why is that not cause for rejoicing?! It is my belief that this is where all healing starts, one heart at a time. I will continue to feel pleased and complimented when I am called a *Pollyanna,* and defend her nature whenever people refer to me in that way intended as a criticism.

Though there may not be easy answers, perhaps there are fairly simple solutions once we become present enough to feel the stillness to know we are one. We hear a great deal about human nature being so dark. And certainly the potential is there within all of us. And yet the human spirit is so naturally resilient and amazing as well. Born to rise up and serve. Our genetic blueprint codes us for connection. We are hardwired to love.

So how do we strike a healthy balance between a self-image that is not prideful arrogance or a sense of complete unworthiness? How do we find our place in the cosmos? It feels like all I know for sure is that it is our life's work to find this place of letting go of labels and comparisons and contests and learn to love from a place where we see each life as magnificent and that we are all in this together.

At a gathering at an ecumenical retreat center called *Camp Brotherhood*, I heard a panel of wonderful speakers from a number of faith traditions express their feelings and a lovely man named Jamal asked us all to "look for the Christ light, the Budda light, the Allah light in everyone. It is the light that we must recognize in each other" he shared with the group assembled. The gathering was celebrating the fortieth anniversary of a peace camp founded by best friends, a Jewish Rabbi, Raphael Levine and a Catholic Priest, William Treacy. With practice, could that recognition of and appreciation for the light *in all* become our way of being in the world?

Humans as a species may possess unique intelligence, but by whose standards? God designed unique intelligence into every life form, and it is respecting the sum total of the holy parts that ultimately allows for the capacity for peace on earth and goodwill for all.

Therefore, I am *holy as thou*. Never holier than, and not less so. *Created* equal. The same. This is not a competition---to be a child of God-----but a sacred gift. Believe it and it is yours, and it cannot be taken away by any means. God loves each of us without conditions. I love this quote from a Sufi sage named Hafiz: *"Everyone is God speaking. Why not be polite and listen to Him?"*

The United States…with liberty and justice for all. What is it that unites us as a nation and as a universe and what divides and destroys us? I offer that it can all be traced back to the belief (or lack of) in the statement that all of us are created equal. And if I see myself as a holy and sacred gift from God, and believe in the truth of that creation, then surely, that is how I see you. If that is how I perceive you to be, then I live in the awareness of offering you the same compassion and care that I am learning to offer myself. Learning, I say, because it is a journey of remembering the love that God blessed us with when we were first kissed into being. And as we come to this awareness as individuals, to offer it as a nation, honoring the nobility of our forefathers' legacy.

I believe that we were all given a multitude of gifts by our Creator. There is a dazzling array of colors and sizes and shapes and textures among humanity and the glorious world of the plant and animal kingdoms and all of creation. So incredibly rich and diverse, we could spend a lifetime just trying to *see* it all, much less get to experience it. It is estimated that we are aware of a mere four percent of what actually exists in the universe! But if we can truly imagine ourselves and all of life as the gift that we are, *what a beginning!*

The church that I love dearly and am devoted to has given so much love in action as service to the world throughout the ages. The body of the church has the potential to be an incredibly powerful source for good. And at the same time, there is the darkness that has been shrouded in unhealthy secrecy where atrocities have been committed both historically and in contemporary times, hidden under the cloak of piety. Perhaps in the *holier than thou* mentality where people become deluded to think that they are above the laws of God. And it is in being willing to shine a light on the broken parts that we find healing. I read a very encouraging book called, *Keep the Faith, Change the Church,* written by representatives from a grassroots group called *The Voice of the Faithful.* The heartfelt intention of this group is to hold individuals in the church who have committed crimes against others and those who have participated in any kind of cover up accountable so that these heinous acts will not continue. At the same time, they are joining with the *vast majority* of church members, both lay and clergy, who are committed to living lives according to the teachings of Jesus. There is also an intention to create more meaningful dialogue between church leadership and lay leaders and helping the important voice of women as equals to continue to emerge, for a purely patriarchal system does not work for any society or family. It must be a healthy dynamic of male and female energies and contribution. When an individual or organization is able to reflect honestly and admit to past mistakes, and ask for forgiveness and create a plan for reconciliation, we as a universal nation are all stronger for it. I am reminded of the powerful quote by a dynamic world citizen hugely ahead of her time, Margaret Mead: *"Never doubt that a small group of thoughtful citizens can change the world; indeed, it's the only thing that ever does."* So my prayers join those of *The Voice of the Faithful* to remain committed to continuing to be guided by the loving and honest, merciful teachings that lead to peace for all.

And since Jesus made his intimate presence known to me as a very small child, I have felt guided to love everyone and everything. Though I have failed miserably at the task many times in countless ways, continue to be propelled forward from that seed planted within me, knowing that as I pick myself up and dust myself off after giving in to fear and judgment, that I am closer to creating beautiful fruit to share with the world. And as I sit with Jesus in the quiet contemplation of my heart, soul and body, I am blessed by the wisdom of the faith traditions of others that are different from mine, yet add to the richness of my life's journey.

It was with a special joy that I read the words of Father William Treacy aloud to my parents as they rested in their recliners from the book that he penned toward the end of the eighth decade of his life called *"He is My Brother."* It describes the rich relationship he enjoyed with his closest friend, Rabbi

Raphael Levine. In one of the chapters, he shares how the rabbi taught the priest the techniques that he learned called *Transcendental Meditation* from the Marharishi Mahesh Yogi himself. Father Treacy shared how learning *TM* considerably strengthened his practice of contemplative prayer and how it has enhanced the commitment to his faith and his life mission to encourage peace for all in the world. *"Imagine that!"* my mother whispered through a smile as she fell asleep and I slipped a bookmarker in the pages and finished for the day. As I tiptoed out of their home, I felt grateful that my parents had always been open minded to teach us to honor all world faith traditions, races and cultures. While serving as a radio officer in the US Navy, my father toured Japan and it left a wonderful impression on him as a place of great beauty. When Dad returned home, he and my mother built a Japanese garden in our backyard and I am confident that we were the only family in our neighborhood in the 1950s attending a Christian church who had a Buddha snow sculpture as well as a Nativity scene in December.

There is no question if we all lined up in a footrace, some could advance to the finish line faster than others. But along the way, some would be the most natural to assist the weary and wounded in a physical sense, and others would come forth to soothe their mental and emotional needs. The spiritual ministers would emerge, as well as those who wanted to nourish us with a sumptuous meal at the end. Naturally, many of them would have grown the food that became the glorious feast and there would be others who would arrange to transport it. And what of the ones who organized and promoted the event in the first place and created the route and all the logistical details that came with it? And the scribes who recorded the myriad stories which arose to nurture and teach those who come after? Who chose to be on the sidelines, offering encouragement, witness and sacred support?

We are all in this footrace to glory together, including those without feet. It was not designed to be a competition, but a celebration of *remembering*. It is, in fact, the human race.

My son Evan is not only related to a founding father of our nation but also has the honor of sharing a birthday with Dr. Martin Luther King, Jr. It is my joyous belief that as a nation and world community that we are *finally* ready to embody the dreams of those great men and all who shared their prayers and visions and sacrificed to make them possible.

And since humans discovered the exquisite beauty of the species known as Equus Caballus thousands of years ago, mankind has dared to create relationships with them and get on their noble backs so that we could fly and race the wind as they do. Many remarkable humans throughout the ages in all countries and cultures have recognized that the horse is a creature that can be a bridge for us between the worlds of the seen and unseen. The tangible and the mysterious. Allowing us to experience Heaven on Earth. They represent our visible life on earth in physical form and also gently guide us to the stillness of the unseen---to our divinity within. If we but allow them. It is through living in deep connection with horses that I am learning to feel my own holiness in ways that I could never have imagined. *And yours.* They have helped me to feel utter humility and meekness as well as incredible strength. They are walking disciples with much to teach in their simple, direct, present moment way of being. And because I am learning to know myself deeply with a new level of health and acceptance, I can offer that to all I encounter. Eleanor Roosevelt stated this truth very simply when she said: *"Friendship with oneself is all important, because without it, one cannot be friends with anyone else in the world."*

These stories from my life are what influenced my beliefs and inner knowledge in a loving God who claims us *all* as gifts. *Everyone is free to choose how to interpret the gift, but it is given nonetheless.* I hope they will touch your heart and help you to remember your own stories and *believe that they can always lead you to love.*

Chapter Two

Nuttier Than a Fruitcake: A Nocturnal Adventure

When writing my first book, I made a deliberate decision to leave out some of my experiences with animals that seemed too far out, even by my own standards of being wide open to the possibilities. Until I established myself with readers as being a rational and highly functional human being, it seemed too risky to be labeled *"nuttier than a fruitcake"* from the get go and have my experiences discounted as the meanderings of a strange albeit pleasant lunatic.

For those of you who have read **Beauty From Brokenness**: *Bits and Pieces of My Journey Into Wholeness*, may I say *Thank You!* Hopefully it was apparent in my writings that I was a conscientious member of society, a calm but vocal animal advocate, loving parent and a trusted friend.

Having said that, I do see the beauty and wonder of the natural world in great detail and listen to the communications I receive daily with a very open mind. Once on the reader board of a local fire department I saw words that said: "Make sure that your mind is not so open that your brains fall out." I chuckled, thinking it might be directed at me, but I would like to defend myself by saying that my mind, brain and gut instincts from my limbic system are becoming in stronger concert every day because of my time spent in the company of horses. Integrating whole brain, whole body rehearsals ultimately produces a rich symphony.

So I decided it was high time to come out of the closet and reveal more of what feels like a two way understanding my animals offer me. They are my direct link to God. My four legged walkie talkies. Horses as Saints.

After the death of our Arabian horse, Ritzy, my mare Chasta was alone to face the holiday that creates tremendous stress for animals: The Fourth of July. Every year I watch in dismay as our domestic pets and wild animals here react in fear and protection to the seemingly constant barrage of firecrackers being set off, even if they are miles away. Everyone's nervous system goes on overdrive, including mine, in spite of the fact I attempt to model quiet acceptance of that which I cannot control and though I love my country with enormous gratitude, I prefer the quiet sounds of nature undisturbed by human explosions.

So since Chasta was solo and likely to have a long and difficult night, I decided to camp outside and keep her company, pulling out my bedroll and chaise lounge and heading to the sand of the round corral. Sharing close quarters at night is always something we have enjoyed together and has strengthened our bonds immensely. I *love* being in nature's nocturnal world in my usually very quiet place on the planet, watching the swallows and bats swoop down on the ponds after insects by the light of the moon, hearing the coos of the mourning doves at the breath of dawn and the outlines of the enormous birds of prey overhead in their craggy places in huge evergreens. The horses are always glad for my company at night and pleased that I consider myself their 24/7 herdmate. Being in their nocturnal world is a special blessing, as if I have been invited to a magical waking dream party that only begins when the sun goes down. The horses are especially calm and tuned in, receptive to quiet co-mingled meditation while I pray and read, sometimes aloud to them and then drift off to sleep.

Basking in the twilight, I propped myself

up with pillows and enjoyed the latest book by master horseman Mark Rashid entitled *Horsemanship Through Life*. Mark is a complete gentleman with horses and people and his books are what I consider enduring classics in this genre. Treat yourself to *anything* he has written.

Chasta was grazing nearby and would occasionally wander over for a scratch and another of the sweet organic baby carrots I kept for her in my pockets. Finally it was getting dark and my eyes were tired so I hollered *"Good night, Chasta, You are magnificent and I love you!"* and pulled up my fabric eye covers that had been hanging around my neck, took a deep breath, said a prayer of gratitude for being out in the fresh air and starlight and settled in for the evening. Though I could feel myself drifting off to sleep, I was also aware of the high pitched incessant buzz of mosquitoes from nearby ponds and could feel them landing on and biting my face. The sweet smelling Citronella and Pennyroyal lotion that I had slathered all over me just wasn't cutting it and my flesh was being eaten alive so I pulled the large wool woven fringed blanket that was covering my sleeping bag up over my head in protection. Shortly after, I was in dreamland in spite of the background noise of the near constant eruption of firecrackers.

It would have been interesting to have been hooked up to a machine that can evaluate at what depth I was asleep, but let's just say, in lay terms, I was "out like a light," something that being outdoors always nurtures for me. That is, until Chasta came along and ripped the blanket back with her teeth with such intensity that I almost fell out of the lounge. Then she proceeded to push her horse lips over my nose, her eyes wild and bugged out, and clamped on, breathing furiously.

I was so shocked and shot full of adrenaline and could not imagine what was happening. I sputtered and flailed until I removed the wet horse lips and teeth that I felt sure had broken my nose. "Chasta, what in the *world* are you doing?!" I shrieked. She stood back and surveyed me warily. "I'm trying to get some rest and I suggest you do the same!" At that hour from a dead sleep I was not long on patience.

She turned and walked away, looking totally insulted and quickly disappeared into the evergreen trees in the darkness. Pulling the wool blanket loosely up over my head again and wiping the horse slobber off my face with my sleeve as only a horse lover can, I went back to sleep in the midst of the booming noise of the fireworks that seemed to surround us at close range.

My peaceful dreams were short lived when Chasta returned, grabbed the blanket in her teeth and again fixed her lips over my face like an equine suction cup. This time her mouth was gaping so wide as to include my chin as she blew with renewed gusto.

Now I am usually not squeamish about being kissed by a horse — in fact, I invite it on a regular basis and consider it part of the territory of loving my animals. Some of my most joyful moments have been up close and personal with soft and slobbery horse muzzles, but *this* was ridiculous! "Chasta *stop!!* I am all out of carrots!" I complained. She leaned back but pricked her ears toward me, scanning me up and down, and looked quite offended but seemed content to walk away.

By now, I had a crick in my neck and was weary from lack of sleep and had a weird adrenaline rush and aches from the head pounding noise of the Fourth of July revelers that continued to blare around me. I let out a huge sigh and for the third time, pulled the blanket over my face and *begged* for rest.

Just as the sun was coming up, Chasta discovered me again and this time pulled the blanket off with such force that it fell to the ground. Before I could prevent it, she clamped on again and there I was thinking that this special night of comforting my horse was a crazy idea at best. Thrashing under her furious breathing, I finally managed to sit up, eye covers askew and fumed, *"OK – that's it, girl!* It's dawn, I'm cold and exhausted, so you're on your own." I am sure that I was quite the picture of elegance with my eye covers up on my forehead, camper's hair and mosquito bitten face slimed with horse drool as I drug my trailing sleeping bag and blanket toward the house. As a final gesture of good will, I reached up to pet her but she turned away, looking disgusted by my hasty exit.

All day I thought about Chasta's strange behavior and chalked it up to her anxiety about the firecrackers and perhaps associating them to her memories of losing the comfort of Ritzy's companionship, especially during stressful times.

Early that evening I left for Wildwood Farm where the new herdmate for Chasta, our sweet young mare named Gaela was in training as part of our purchase agreement that this young and worried rescue horse would be lovingly restarted to give her a new and confident beginning. No one could have done a better job than a natural horsewoman named Sarah Cassatt, for which I am truly

grateful. I observed and sometimes participated in the sessions but on this evening, it
was so warm that I just wanted to take her to
find some shade. Putting on a rope halter, I
led her down the hill toward the coolness of
the wooded trails.

Gaela had been uncomfortable initially with
having me on her right side, so I was leading her there with that in mind to help her
find relaxation with it, placing myself at
her barrel making certain that she could see
and feel me back there by keeping the lead
rope in my right hand and stroking her belly
and withers with my left as we walked. She
sighed and relaxed, so I stroked her some
more and moved up to her right shoulder.
She was keeping her stride in perfect sync
with mine and her eye was soft and relaxed.
As I felt myself release my breath, I noticed
her watching me intently and that is when I
heard the words as if she had spoken them
into my ear. *"She thought you were dead!"*

"Huh?!" I looked around to see where the
voice was coming from. We remained alone
together, a good distance from other humans
on this vast acreage.

Then it clicked. Chasta! The blanket! I looked
at Gaela to see if I was on the right track. She

gave me a look that smacked of *"Duh!"* and suddenly it all made sense.

When Ritzy died, he was lying peacefully on the ground and after my son had kissed his forehead for the final time, he had put a small wool saddle blanket over it to ease his own pain from the haunting image of his beloved horse's rigid face and the yet open eyes after death. Chasta had approached us slowly and while I laid over Ritzy's body covered by a large wool fringed blanket, she pulled the small one off his face with her teeth and had blown in to his stilled nostrils wildly for the better part of an hour, off and on. She licked and blew in cycles, apparently attempting loving and life saving resuscitation. Finally, in exhausted defeat, she lowered her head completely to the ground and then raised it to the Heavens and trumpeted a shrill and heart wrenching blast that proclaimed his passage and stood in sacred vigil over his lifeless body.

When our neighbor came with his backhoe to bury our beloved friend, Chasta and I watched in quiet reverence and wild grief as his body lay at the bottom of the huge grave that had been dug under an old growth Fir tree where Ritzy had loved to rest in life. Taking the blanket off of my shoulders that had been covering his body after his death when he laid on the ground, I gave it to our friend, Doyle, who waited kindly while we said our final goodbyes. Then he carefully covered Ritzy's body with it and we backed up and watched him fill the tremendous hole he had dug with his machine.

The wool blanket was a woven Mexican design of stripes, *exactly* like the one I had covering my body and face the night Chasta woke me repeatedly with her wild eyed breathing. The last time she had seen a blanket like that, it was covering the face and dead body of her lifemate and best friend. She had tried valiantly to restore his life but it was too late.

When she saw me lying there on the chaise, my face and body covered with the same material, did she think that I was dead, too, and that she could resuscitate me? That was the message Gaela seemed to transmit to me, loud and clear, walking together with a strong relaxed connection. Does God use the trees and the wind and animals to touch our hearts so deeply that we become tuned into the mystery of the oneness of all life? That we *know* and *understand* that we know because we are vibrating at a frequency that is attuned to our Creator?

I returned home that night after my evening with Gaela and found Chasta waiting for me at the gate. Approaching her with a slow and deliberate pace, I greeted her softly with a quiet voice and said, "*Thank you, my friend.* I apologize for giving you such a fright and not being aware and grateful for your heroic attempts to help me. Please be patient with me. I am learning to listen and observe and feel with my heart, and with your help, it will become my true nature."

She responded by putting her face down to my nostrils and breathed into them as softly as a kitten and without a trace of slobber.

Chasta at the gate

Photo by Glen Bartlett

Chapter Three

Caution: Open Mind Required

Okay…here we go again! I will start this story with a "pre-claimer": *Please read with a completely open mind.* If you experience your eyes glazing over and you hear yourself dismissing me as an eccentric who has lost her way or feel like burning me at the stake, either skip this and move on or consider just opening yourself to the possibilities. All I know is that I am retelling my own experience from the vantage point of my perceptions of reality. And believe me, this is a s-t-r-e-t-c-h for my mind, too. Yet for my heart and soul, it feels amazing and hopeful and quite beautiful because I believe that as I heal and grow more aware of the goodness of God, so do all of you. I am convinced that we are all in this wild and wooly thing called life together as we greet each new experience.

It is difficult to know where this story begins, as is true for all life since each of us has a never ending story yearning to be told and understood---we are *not* our stories---rather we are living spirits---but in the physical world, how our lives unfold is of great importance. We experience our reality one moment at a time and what each of us has to share is very rich, indeed.

My sister, Debbie, was born to our parents at very tender ages when our father was away on a ship in the US Navy overseas. Shortly after he finished his commitment of service to his country and was home with his young wife and baby, our mother became pregnant with me and I was born when Debbie was just fifteen months old.

At that time in their lives, my parents had very limited finances, so when I emerged into the family, it displaced Debbie from her crib, high chair and buggy---virtually her physical world---and she was expected, however unintentionally at the time, to become a big sister to me rather than the true babe that she actually was.

Needless to say, those circumstances did not always bring out the nurturer in my sister, even though that is one of her most beautiful, natural and glorious traits. Watching her love and guide her young grandson in present time moves me deeply---they share a bond that few souls ever have the privilege to experience.

In fact, as the barely toddling baby that she was, Debbie felt clearly upset. Discussions of a *new* baby arriving soon left her so disturbed that our concerned parents purchased a life sized doll for her to love on the advice of our pediatrician which represented a months worth of groceries that she promptly took by one arm and flung cross the room, hitting the wall.

Fast forward to the summer when we were six and seven. Debbie and I *loved* horses, as many girls that age do. On every special occasion possible, we met our cousins at the *Lake Serene Pony Farm* near our home and took trail rides on the dependable mounts there that left me giddy with delight and then got to spend our dollar (usually a birthday present) at their gift shop packed full of horsey things with the big mullioned window that invited you in. For me it was always one of the pot metal horses that I lined up on the windowsill of my bedroom so that I could see them before I feel asleep and dreamed of flesh and blood horses. The desire was to have one miniature figure of every color for your own personal herd that fed my rich fantasy life.

That Christmas our grandmother gifted Debbie with a weeklong camp at *The Flying Horse-*

shoe Ranch, in Ellensburg, Washington, several hundred miles from our home. She also received cowgirl boots, hat, jeans, a western shirt and bandana. I was *devastated.* In my heart, I *knew* that I was at least as horse crazy as Debbie, and if it was a contest, I would have argued that I could whinny louder and shake my mane more dramatically. (Never mind that I had a short 'pixie' haircut and Debbie had long, luxurious golden curls...!) Certainly I drew detailed horses with more frequency and saw them running through my dreams continuously.

As the date to leave approached, my mood became more sullen and the entire time she was gone, I could feel little happiness for her incredible experience in my perceived state of exclusion.

When we went to pick her up, I got to meet the horse that she had been able to choose *to be her very own for the week.* His name was Jet because he was dark as night and absolutely gorgeous. For Heavens sake, he looked like *Black Beauty!* I had a vivid, aching memory of standing with my heart touching his, smelling the unmatched sweet scent of a sweaty horse in the sunshine, feeling incredibly sad and *un*-chosen.

None of this was intentional, of course. No adult set out to deliberately wound me, nor did my innocent yet incredibly lucky sister! When I queried my mother about this in recent years as an adult about why my grandmother did not include me, she said that since Debbie was the oldest that it must have made sense to her mother at the time. Then she went on to tell me that she remembered times when she had the same feelings when her older sister was given special gifts and privileges that she had not received, not then or ever.

This was never discussed until I was given my Palomino colored mare, Chasta, as a midlife gift and she shook up my entire world—literally and in every way. Enough to write my first book about her in vivid detail. Fairly early in our experiences together, Chasta erupted in a leaping physical display of motion that had me both awed and fearful. In that moment, I had a flashback memory of my sister Debbie and her golden hair and formidable presence in motion. It was clear to me that God had given me Chasta to revisit what I needed to heal for I had deeply bonded with her yet remained anxious in her presence at times. As siblings, my sister and I had a similar relationship over the years.

Debbie is a very talented licensed massage therapist. She is incredibly intuitive and knowledgeable, using both hemispheres of her brain equally to put feel and skill into her hands. One day she was giving me a relaxing massage when the memory of the emotions brought to the surface by Chasta's big reactions gave me the courage to share my heart and I suddenly blurted out what I had experienced with Chasta and that her big wounded female blonde form made me realize she was a gift for both of us. I told Debbie that I had felt like myself as a small child feeling huge big sister energy in Chasta's presence and that she had come to help me work through the old conflicts and feelings of powerlessness.

Debbie stopped and withdrew her hands and I noticed that she looked rather taken aback since I had opened my eyes with this impulsive revelation. As our eyes met, she looked at me tenderly and leaned down to hug me and we enjoyed a long embrace in silence before she resumed the healing touch of massage on the muscles of my legs.

Though Debbie and I both have habitual patterns of compulsive chattering (that we are both working on individually to change through awareness and practice), during a massage we are usually mute by deliberate intent. It felt eerily quiet after my outburst of emotion and revelation and our tender embrace and suddenly she broke the silence and exclaimed, *"Wow!*---you have *so much* held tension in this area!" followed by abruptly flinging back the sheet that discretely covers a person's body during a therapeutic massage and declaring "For heavens sake, you're my *sister!* May I touch you here?!" She had her fingers on the muscle between my inner thigh and pelvic area----a place on the body where a massage therapist does not ordinarily go. I nodded in permission and she started pressing in almost a bouncing motion off and on that caused me to tighten in wincing pain. "Relax and allow yourself to feel like it is a rubber band," she advised. I took a deep breath as she bounced vigorously and felt myself gradually feeling elastic rather than rigid in that area. The intense discomfort became sweet release. Then she repeated the same procedure on the other side.

The rest of the massage was quiet and relaxing but we had both experienced a breakthrough---one she had facilitated for me as a loving---if not yet formidable---big sister. Later I was sore but had incredibly improved ease of movement in my pelvic area and the next day I went horseback riding with friends and both sat and posted the trot better than I ever had before. Chasta and I were repeating the tenderness and harmony that Debbie and I had experienced.

Time passed and I continued to enjoy strengthening my relationships with my beautiful blonde sister and my gorgeous golden horse. Our church family was planning an auction fundraiser for a pilgrimage trip to Italy for our son Evan's youth group. One evening I was at a meeting to catalog items which had been donated when I picked up an envelope that said, "Guest Ranch Weekend" and opened it to find a brochure from *The Flying Horseshoe*--- the ranch where my sister had gone nearly fifty years before! I held it in disbelief, emotional memories flooding me. "*Where* did this come from?!" I wondered aloud and was told that it was donated by the same family that still owns the ranch several generations later---their grandson had been a college roommate with one of our favorite young parishioners who had been responsible for the acquisition.

When I went home, I looked for the tiny photo that showed me standing next to Debbie's black horse, Jet, from the week at the camp, from the only small photo album that exists from my childhood. It is a black and white square image, taken with a Brownie camera from the fifties. After taking it in to a photo shop to be enlarged so that you could really see the expression on my face, it amazed me how vivid the memory felt. I showed it to my son, Evan, and he responded with a startled "*Whoa, Mom!* You were *so sad* in this picture---what was going on for you?" I shared the story but told him that "that was then and this is now" and reminded him how grateful I felt in the present moment for having our own horses to love.

A month later I attended a workshop at Sandra Wallin's *Chiron's Way Centre* that was facilitated by Marijke Van de Water, an expert equine homeopath and nutritionist, author of *Healing Horses Their Way!* , who is a remarkably intuitive animal communicator. It was an incredible experience and continued to stretch my belief system about what is possible between species and my own intuitive abilities.

Less than a week after I returned home, our beloved Arabian horse, Ritzy, did not recover from a bewildering illness in spite of all of our healing intentions that left us all absolutely devastated. Chasta's closest friend, her lifemate, was buried in soil that the two of them used to stand together on to relax in the shade of the giant old growth Fir trees overhead there.

Plunged into deep grief, the wet, cold weather of the winter season seemed to mirror my emotions. Ritzy's passing affected me deeply and I felt his spirit presence encouraging my old held emotions of sadness to be fully realized so that I could release them. I was truly concerned about Chasta who was definitely struggling with her own profound grief as well.

The situation prompted me to consult with Marijke, who does long distance healing communication based on photos of your animals. She started by asking me some questions and after a few minutes she told me that Chasta was struggling with a black horse form named Jet that represented our grief that she held in her heart space which she had received from mine that she was trying to release for me. I asked her to repeat her statement to make sure that I had heard it accurately since it seemed too complex and a little weird to wrap my mind around. She told me that Chasta needed help with this and to rest comfortably while she worked with her. Feeling strangely heavy and sleepy, I thanked Marijke and hung up.

When I awoke from my dreamy state, suddenly I thought of my old aching sadness that I felt when I looked at the picture of my heart pressed up against Jet's heart at the ranch all those years ago in my brief encounter with him. I got out the enlarged photo and sat up staring at it. *Was it possible* that I had carried this sadness in my heart energetically and that Chasta truly had been attempting to absorb and release it for me? Surely I had spent countless hours with my heart also pressed into hers!

"A black horse form named Jet," Marijke had clearly stated. How could she have possibly known that I had ever had an encounter with a black horse named Jet that had been associated with sadness all those years ago that had just coincidentally re-emerged when the auction donation had caused me to enlarge and study and revisit those emotions? And when I did, how tender I felt about the image of our mother, so young and beautiful, always trying to make life 'fair' for her children, when it is seldom or ever possible. Behind my mother all you can see of Debbie are the cowgirl boots and jeans that she is wearing that I had coveted so desperately!

Oh, how unresolved emotions can trap us in the past! My sister was an innocent horse crazy seven year old herself who deserved to have a time to shine connecting with a beautiful black horse named Jet.

Eckhart Tolle describes in his landmark book, *A New Earth – Awakening to Your Life's Purpose*, the unresolved emotions of the ego creating what he calls a *'pain body'* that becomes an energetic pattern of cellular memory that affects our behavior. Unless we recognize the unhealthy egoic patterns of the mind and realize they are merely thoughts and therefore have no power over us, we can continue to be distracted and governed by them. Bravo to Oprah Winfrey for creating an interactive worldwide webcast to share Mr. Tolle's profound insights.

How did Marijke access that information from the field of energy that connects us all? One of the most fascinating books that I have ever been riveted to while reading is called *The Field,* by Lynn McTaggart, which describes in detail the science and the mysticism that explains and supports both the mystery of faith and the energetic interconnectedness of the universe. It will expand your understanding of life by reading of the experiments about consciousness by many of the most brilliant humans on the planet. Lynn has accomplished an incredible service by compiling this compelling and fascinating research.

Did these emotions of sadness and feeling rejected become a part of a *'pain body'* in me that moved energetically from my heart to the heart of a black horse named Jet who absorbed my incredible heartfelt longing for him and somehow remained in me until a golden horse came into my life and felt my longing rekindled? Did my love for her and our mutual grief in our loss of Ritzy's physical presence come full circle so that we could be healed? Discovering the old memory of the ranch and the photo and taking Marijke's class all in a timeline that led to transformation? The light of God always leads us out of darkness and Eckhart Tolle reminds us that the power of that light resides in the *Now* of the present moment.

As we begin to have Divine presence permeate our consciousness more frequently, the pain bodies that formed from old perceived wounds dissolve and transmute into the energy that can heal us, creating the space where peace resides.

When I sent Marijke a copy of the old photo, she was able to better understand what she recognized in her energetic reading and assured me that the mission had been accomplished. *With God, all things are possible and the possibilities are infinite.*

*Ahhhhhh…*The deep peace that comes from experiencing the mystery of faith is a balm for my spirit and now what I feel when I look beyond the pain in this photo is the deep and unending interconnectedness. What do *you* experience?

All parties are innocent…

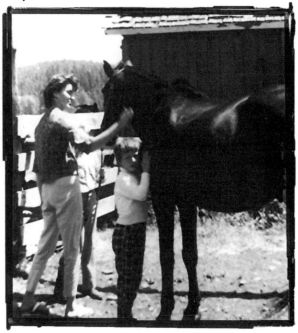

Chapter Four

Your Slip is Showing

The process of writing my first book resulted in typos galore. Mistakes happen, of course, but it became ridiculous, as if at night when the lights were out, they were multiplying exponentially like rabbits. Proofreading is a challenging task and it can create a condition where one's eyes glaze over, cross, and roll back in their sockets, usually in the wee hours of the night. Especially if you are re-reading it for the umpteenth time and were *certain* that you made those corrections the last run through.

By the time my manuscript was ready to be published, I felt like there had been countless outtakes, as those following a feature film in the movie theatre, but this was more than the editing that caused material to hit the cutting room floor.

These were slips in the Freudian sense. When I meant one thing and said another, at least how my fingers typed it into the word processor. There were many times when I felt strong emotions as I typed only to look up moments later to see that what was emphatic to me was printed inadvertently in all capital letters on the screen. The same for italics and bold features---they seemed to have mind of their own as well.

The technical term for a Freudian slip is *Parapraxis*: an error in speech, memory or physical action caused by the unconscious mind---often a verbal mistake that is thought to reveal an unconscious belief, thought or emotion.

As a writer, mine came out in word form on the pages. I was describing trail rides, something that I love to do on horseback, but it came out as *trial* rides, as did the expression, Happy Trails, which became *Happy Trials!* Anyone who has ever had a mishap on the trails knows that trials can emerge in a heartbeat. But beautiful wooded trails, knowledge as a horseman, and a solid sense of humor are a great combination for the trials we all inevitably face. And we can inadvertently cause them to happen when we carry our trials with us in our tense minds, seat and hands. I have truly found that the glorious trails are a fantastic place to leave my trials behind, allowing them to evaporate into the fresh air and be carried by the winds to become a part of the composted thicket that we crunch over.

Actually, this process of making so many mistakes and learning to correct them has been a valuable asset to my work/play with horses and vice versa. I have developed a new level of comfort with mistakes in general as I increase my skills handling ropes and hit myself in the face or trip over what is under my feet less frequently. There is a greater sense of where I am in time and space because the horses have helped to ground me as well as facilitate my movement. Also, there is the speed versus accuracy ratio. I can only type as fast as I can think. With horses, if you don't have harmony at the walk, there is no way it will be there at the canter. Master horseman Pat Parelli says: *"Slow and right beats fast and wrong."* It's true. Finding a rhythm and pace where I remain aware allows me to stay relaxed, yet focused.

Returning to my many slips of the tongue/pen/keyboard, there were all of my *fiends* (who shall remain nameless) instead of *friends*. And, of course, I wisely advised that we all need to be our own *best fiend!* Usually that is a big part of the problem---we seldom treat ourselves the way we would like to be treated.

Here is one that is truly fascinating — I typed *unties* when *unites* was intended---the seeming opposite. Sometimes the line is very fine between polarities. On this same vein, there was *scared* when I meant *sacred*. How often and easily we can miss the divineness of life when burdened by fear. Surrendering to the sacred is our release.

Or *Sinday* instead of *Sunday.* Now there is an ironic name for the Sabbath and one that Freud would have a field day with. How easily we can stray from the trail and get lost! And speaking of sin, old Dr. Sigmund Freud was pretty sure that most everything was skewed and repressed sexuality. He seemed to be obsessed with these ideas and decided that a woman's attraction to horses was somehow deviant. He suggested that horses represented a substitute for men, power and sex.

I and countless other females have news for Dr. Freud! Just ask the lovely Leah Juarez of Equesse, Inc. She publishes a website and magazine devoted to the special relationships women have with horses. Horses help us to connect with the intuitive nature of our subconscious mind where we find our deepest self and our true nature as women who can learn to love men in healthy ways by understanding and embracing our own personal power and sexuality. So horses make ideal couples counselors and men who lovingly support their female partners in their devotion to horses reap big rewards because they know a woman's heart. *We all want our hearts to be known.*

Photo by Erich Tritz

Amelia Tritz and her horses, Mariner and Jewel

Freud is quoted as saying: *"The mind is like an iceberg. It floats one seventh of its bulk above water."* In other words, most of what drives us is below the surface of our awareness.

And as far as I am concerned, horses make the best therapists to help us tap into those depths. Freud wisely said: *"the doctor should be opaque to his patients, and like a mirror, should show them nothing but what is shown to him."* Which is precisely what horses do for us. They are walking MRI machines with hair. They read the energy of our emotions and know what we feel and help us get in touch with it. I also believe that horses have the ability to read our holographic blueprint and can help us by holding a mirror to ourselves so that we can become our own inner *physical* healer/physician. And spiritual advisor. Not to mention mental health counselor.

Humans often say one thing and mean another. Not so with horses. They say what they mean and mean what they say, usually without any sound effects. This helps the humans get in touch with our inner non-verbal knowing that is beyond thought forms. Albert Einstein said: *"The intuitive mind is a sacred gift and the rational mind is the faithful servant. We have created a society that favors the servant and has forgotten the gift."*

So it is no surprise that women (and, of course, men who are on a path to self-discovery) are deeply attracted to these incredibly perceptive animals who can reintroduce us to ourselves, rid our lives of inner baggage and find the peace, joy and connection we all yearn for.

This is why the movement of Equine Guided Development/Therapy has become so widespread and successful. Visionaries and leaders in the field like Barbara Rector, Linda Kohanov, and Sandra Wallin have helped to blaze trails by developing teaching systems that others can follow. Individuals can choose to study the path as a profession or as a participant---either one on one or with groups. The combination of skilled humans, balanced in intellect and instinct, partner with the master therapists in the form of horses. *Walking the Way of the Horse: Exploring the Power of the Horse Human Relationship* by Leif Hallberg is a must read and invaluable resource. The reason these programs enjoy successful transformations is due to the integrative approach of supporting the whole person----body, mind, spirit and emotions while doing the same for the horse as a collaborative partner. This is the new paradigm for health where integration from the best of allopathic medicine combines with complementary practices that support all aspects of wellness. Traditional medical schools are even using this model of working with horses for students to help them learn the art of diagnosis and treatment options through skills learned in the workshops where they employ their knowledge from textbooks as they enhance their "gut hunches." Physician, heal thyself. And, true to the Hippocratic oath: *First, do no harm.* Horses are true integrative health specialists—and Hippocrates himself knew that.

Dr. Freud, at the end of his career, in total exasperation wrote: *"The great question that has never been answered, and which I have not been able to answer, despite my thirty years of research into the female soul, is: What does a woman want?"*

Dare I say she wants the deep connection with all of life that a horse can offer by telling her that: *"Your slip is showing"* whenever she is not fully congruent? Brought back to center from this awareness, she exhales deeply, smiles as she strokes her four-legged teacher, and says a prayer of thanks.

Photos by Jaye Nichols

Kathy Yaeger and her soul mate, Tango

"Dr Freud... *You should have been a horse!"*

Photo by Marion Cox, Images of the Divine Equine

Chapter Five

Beyond Boredom

My sister and I, wearing cut off jeans that we had proudly fringed ourselves, were spending a hot summer day in our suburban backyard with two friends from our junior high school, one of whom had just declared that she was bored. *Hopelessly bored.* She was the most privileged among us materially by a long shot and led a very pampered life.

Not sure I had ever felt bored before, I listened to her shrill whining attentively. "There's nothing to do! I am so bored!" It seemed reasonable, maybe even a little *daring* to feel bored. After all, she was thirteen and seemed so grown up and sophisticated to me at twelve, so I looked at the others, shrugged and echoed their refrain. "We're bored!" was our battle cry that we took to my mother, who was inside sorting laundry. Barely glancing in our direction, Mom replied with, "Bored?! Well, hop in the car!"

Wow! *That* was easy! Where were we headed? To the ice cream parlor? The ice skating rink? The four of us clueless adolescents were chattering so fast and furiously that we hardly noticed my mother in the car much less what direction we were heading until we arrived at an unfamiliar gated entry that led to a driveway that came to a series of dismal looking buildings. Mom pulled up in our white Pontiac station wagon to what appeared to be an office. With the windows rolled down in the summer heat, we were aware of an unpleasant odor even from inside the car. Before any of us could form words, a tall emaciated male form came into view, swinging his long arms in spastic movements as he shouted intermittently, somewhere between an unintelligible shriek and groan. He was heading in our direction. Our chattering had long since ceased and now we were all pop eyed as Mom casually said, "*Hop out*, girls!" and headed resolutely for the entrance.

The young man had passed us and we could still hear his incomprehensible sounds echoing in the stillness of the muggy air. It seemed like there was no option but to follow, so we walked mutely up the steps, single file and weak in the knees. Once inside, we clung to each other silently in confusion as my Mother asked brightly for the director and announced, "these girls have time on their hands and would like to volunteer!" Stunned, we looked at the man who shook hands with my Mother briefly before she headed for the exit, saying she would return for us at the end of the day.

The director sized us up and certainly could see that we were as surprised as he was to meet us. Wisely, after introducing himself, he said he would give us a tour of the facilities, which turned out to be an institution for the mentally and physically disabled. And it was only a few miles from our *boring* home! Obviously none of us had any idea that it existed and had no frame of reference for what we were about to see.

If we thought the strong unpleasant odor in the outside air was disturbing, once inside the building, it became intense and overpowering. It smelled of urine and feces, body odor and strong pine scented disinfectant. The rooms were small and hot and the surfaces old and dingy. The director was matter of fact when he told us that most of the residents in this ward had severe mental and physical handicaps. He walked briskly ahead with the four of us following in a bug eyed trance as we saw patients lying on beds, rubber mats on the floor and large home-made looking playpens. It was difficult to tell, especially without staring, if they were male or female, young or old. Many of them had severe hydrocephalus, the fluid engorging their heads in grotesque forms unlike anything I had ever seen. There would be absolutely no way their bodies could support the weight of the skull if upright, so that appeared to be the extent of their lives, lying there, diapered, drooling and seemingly incoherent. As huge as their distended heads had become, most of them had elongated limbs that were skeletally thin by comparison.

My heart pounded so hard that I thought it would break as tears filled my eyes, and ran down my hot cheeks. "Some of these residents are fortunate enough to have families who visit, but many do not," our tour guide remarked while the staff members we saw perused us curiously and went about their business as the director led us out of that building toward another. As relieved as I felt leaving that place of haunting images, I felt as desperate to help them as I did to walk away.

"I think the recreation center would be a good place for you girls to start---the residents who can use this facility have greater mobility." By now, the four of us were ghostly pale and I felt dizzy and nauseated.

We walked into an old room with a makeshift gym and various pieces of sporting equipment, noticing a number of residents milling around, looking at us expectantly. The director took us into a smaller room around the corner and introduced us to very small woman whose name was Carol. "These young ladies would like to volunteer their time," he declared, then turned on his heel and walked away just like my Mother had earlier.

We looked at Carol. She looked at us. Her movements were spasticated and her speech was slurred and indistinct. Since none of us could understand what she was trying to express, I had the bright idea to see if she wanted to join the others. "Would you like to play basketball? I offered tentatively. Being twelve, my heart was in the right place with no intention to patronize. Carol started in again, even more slowly and deliberately, raising her voice in frustration, "*I* am *not* a r-e-s-i-d-e-n-t!" we *finally* heard.

She was the director of the recreational program and had driven her specially equipped car to work! Her disease, Cerebral Palsy, imposed severe physical disabilities, but she had the mental capacity to be a wonderfully efficient employee. *Talk about an emotional roller coaster.* Carol was clearly offended by our innocent judgements and we were equally sheepish, especially me, after tripping over my tongue with my unintentionally condescending suggestion, but then softened and told us that she was glad we came and showed us around.

By the end of the day, we were very relieved to see Mom, knowing that we could return to the comfort of our sheltered lives. *But we were changed.* Our world had expanded. We understood compassion on an entirely new level. There was a great big world out there beyond our suburban backyard and much of it was difficult and immensely challenging. Yet truly rewarding and strangely comforting. A profound gratitude for our lives developed overnight which did not prevent us from behaving like the immature adolescents that we were, but we had been robbed of our innocence in a manner intended to help us--- we were *different.*

Yet now as an adult looking back from this stage of my growth, was my Mother's choice to expose us to this lesson and press us into service harsh? Is it comparable to an adult throwing a child into the deep end of a pool to teach them to swim? Does the end justify the means if the intended result causes trauma to others? Could I have developed the same level of compassion in a more nurturing way? She exposed us to this experience in a way that had been modeled for her. Questions to ponder.

After summer ended and our classes resumed at school, we started a committee to sponsor residents without family or friends to set up visits. Students came out in groups to play games at the recreation center, make crafts, and share time with others less fortunate. The newspaper did a story and ran a photograph of the girls who started the program. It should have been of my Mother, with her intentions for good. Or the director for choosing that profession. Or Carol, for the courage that defined her life.

Interestingly, hippotherapy, which is physical therapy for humans on horseback is one of the most significantly effective modalities for patients with Cerebral Palsy. It has been scientifically demonstrated that the cadence of the gaits of a horse has a dramatic ability to increase muscle strength, mobility and balance in the human. And the mental and emotional component of the joy and freedom of being connected with these noble animals has a major healing effect as well. I will be bold to suggest that the horses provide a spiritual gateway to God also, with no doubt in my heart and soul that they are angelic messengers.

A friend of mine described a wonderful and typical story about the value of equine therapy and how well suited horses are to the task, how tuned in they are to their purpose. She cares for a young child with severe Cerebral Palsy who looks forward to his weekly sessions with eagerness and delight. Extremely small and frail, she tells me that he beams with joy the entire time he is in the presence of horses. One time as she sat in the bleachers during his therapy session, the horse handler became distracted and was hollering across the arena to another employee when the saddle started to slip and the child tipped precariously. My friend noticed that the horse, a gentle sorrel chestnut named Buck, stopped immediately, squared up and adjusted his body to balance the tiny boy.

The handler tugged on the horse's lead to ask him to keep moving without turning around to assess the situation but the horse refused to budge. Only when the human therapist looked back in exasperation did she see why the devoted and intelligent horse therapist did not obey her suggestion. She stopped, corrected the tack, reassured her little charge and praised the horse lavishly, promising in the future to always give her full attention to each horse and human pair. And to *always* provide appropriate assistants to help.

Another woman I met at a benefit for horse rescue introduced me to her lovely daughter who had recently graduated from high school and was on her way to college to study natural horsemanship with a desire to create a future filled with horses to share them with others after all they had given her in her young life. Her mother explained to me later when she was away riding in a demonstration that she had been a Chernobyl baby who had the characteristic failure to thrive symptomatic of a lack of early bonding. Her adopted Mother told me through tears of joy that her beautiful daughter had literally come alive when they started her in equine therapy---that the horses had awakened her spirit and given her the passion that was at the center of her world, and now she was prepared to make horses her livelihood so she could do the same for others.

So, because of my own Mother's wisdom in

action on that hot summer day many years ago, I have never felt the sensation of being bored since. *Ever.*

Instead, I was taught by example to engage in life, not shrink back in complacency. Not in this remarkable world we live in where there is always something amazing to learn and experience, however much it calls on every bit of your strength and commitment. Especially with horses around! *Thanks,* Mom. And thank *you,* Chasta, for showing me how to find deep connection in a greater level of awareness without my good intentions creating undue trauma for all involved. I am *learning.*

> *"The cure for boredom is curiosity.*
> *There is no cure for curiosity."*
> Ellen Parr

Heart to Heart

Jacob discovers "My Pony!"

Personal Ponies Ltd. is an incredible blessing in the lives of countless children and seniors. For more information, visit www.personalponies.org

Photos courtesy of Sandra Seiden, Florida State Director of Personal Ponies Ltd.

Chapter Six

Trashtrap

I have always had a prudish aversion to the f-word. It just sounds absolutely rude and crude to me, and if I were to defend my position, it makes a mockery, or worse, an attack on something that was designed to be sacred. Humans fall short of God's designs in a lot of areas and for this word to permeate our culture to the extent that is does is a perfect example. Hearing females use it feels especially distasteful to me---it doesn't seem at all empowering to listen to the liberal use of it by my 'sisters' of any age. It does not inspire me to become a better woman or elevate my role in my community or society at large.

A friend whose observations I greatly admire shared with me that it is indeed a matter of cultural acceptance since she witnessed a group of silver haired senior women in Eastern Canada with brooches at their throats and hankies scented with lavender at their bosoms peppering their speech with the word that I so distain as if it were a very useful and ordinary adjective. That seems truly amazing to me! *Little old ladies!!!*

Yet since I *do* live in a civilized culture, at least to some extent, I think we really need to examine and reserve words that evoke strong emotion for times when they will, indeed, have an impact, rather than becoming so common as to no longer hear them. Or to use them to the point that we become completely desensitized to how vulgar we sound. Is being vulgar a sign of strength? Or power? *Not to me.*

Fortunately I have friends who like me well enough to save me from my rigid, prudish ways when they interfere with my ability to grow. Or laugh. Like the time when my pal Megan gave me my first book written by Anne Lamott. "You *have* to read this!" she said as she held the hardcover close to her breast, like a treasure. "Just close your eyes when you see the f-word because she is a *fantastic* writer!"

Anne Lamott, indeed, is one of the most expressive writers of our times, in my humble yet experienced opinion, since I have been reading eclectically with a voracious appetite since words first danced across a page for me as a child. The ability to evoke an emotional response is my best evaluation of the skills of a writer. You could open any title by Lamott to a random page and there will be something, *or a lot of things*, that will resonate with you enough to command your attention, and quite often precipitate a belly laugh that rumbles throughout your being and makes your day, causing you to feel thankful to be alive. And more often than not, it is *wickedly* funny, as in things that caused me to howl when they are not something one should laugh at in polite company.

One morning over tea as I read Anne's delicious and daunting primer for writers, *Bird by Bird*, I laughed out loud so hard that all three dogs at my feet awoke from their slumber to see what they were missing. Before I could recover from my hysteria, I had to run to the bathroom quickly to relieve myself of the tea.

And it is Anne (evoking the fiendish laughter in me has us on a first name basis now, you will notice) who inspired me to go back and take snapshots of the vignettes that my mind has recorded over time of the sweet and poignant moments or the haunting and painful ones and everything in between worth remembering. It is learning to accept and live with that balance of light and dark that assures us our humanity--our place.

Like the year we moved from our suburban home in the metropolitan area of the Northwest to our summer place ninety minutes north in a small rural community on the coast.

If truth be told, we moved primarily for two reasons. And they are *biggies.* First, the area directly north of our weekend-summer home was designated to become the site of a nuclear power plant. It was proposed to be situated on a pristine island adjacent to one of the most visited locations of natural beauty in the world, *Deception Pass.* My parents decided we would join the good fight to change the minds of the powers that be and at least enjoy the property if it were not possible to reverse the ill advised and environmentally devastating decision. My younger sister, Wendy, was a peaceful protester that Halloween, complete with a tie-dyed shirt, a necklace Mom made from beach shells and a sign that quietly implored, *"Save Skagit Bay!"*

And second, and also tragically, my uncle had taken his own life that summer at the age of sixteen. My grandmother moved out of the home where his sudden and violent death occurred and into ours. We moved to the beach.

Being an adolescent who is wrestling with the emotional turmoil of fitting in and being accepted and trying not to have your sanitary pad flip over as you walked self consciously from class to class is enough without adding those *huge* adjustments.

Writing this caused me to suddenly remember that sanitary pads used to require a little stretchy belt to keep them in place, long before the self-adhesive varieties hit the market! One more little discomfort to twist and chafe while I was trying desperately to feel cool---or at least *look* cool. Those are the little details that Lamott is talking about when she invites writers to dig! *Excavate!*

Within weeks, I had attended the unexpected and untimely funeral of a member of our family who had been a huge part of our lives, witnessed the devastated responses of my grandmother whose only son had made that final, bitter choice, and moved away from the home that I had grown up in, all without benefit of any counseling, professional or otherwise. My uncle was only two years older than me so he was more like a big brother. One that I looked up to and had a case of adolescent hero worship for. Those were the days before feelings were invited to be expressed and children went to grief counselors.

I just remember a line up of pretty girls, high school classmates, putting single red roses on his casket, while I stood nearby, trembling and mute but for choking on my own tears. I had known and loved him all of my life. Where was *my* rose? Why was *I* not in that line?

My siblings and I were enrolled in the local small schools, and because we lived outside the transportation area, needed to be driven to the closest bus stop. Meeting the neighboring families with school aged children, we agreed to carpool.

My older sister, Debbie, in some kind of advanced puberty protest, had locked herself in the bathroom and dyed her hair peroxide blonde. She accidentally botched the job and it came out an electric shade of apricot. Not quite as daring, I had decided it was high time to start shaving my legs, so found the nearest razor and proceeded to inadvertently cut myself to ribbons, not the exciting and sophisticated rite of passage I had imagined it to be! My brother, Craig, was in such a growth spurt that he had to keep raisins and peanuts in his pockets to prevent dizzy spells as a result of low blood sugar. He was growing so fast that it wasn't long before his back to school jeans were a tad bit too short.

Debbie and I wore hotpants and mini skirts---hers being suede with a star stitched on the back pocket from which tendrils of fringe hung down from, and fortunately, I had shimmering tights to cover my razor scabby legs, since my dress did not.

On the days our sainted mother drove, we headed up the road to pick up the kids who lived in the sturdy brick house their German father had built, himself a mason. They were quiet children, smelling of potato pancakes, and though their mother was always pleasant when we came to pick them up, she looked mortified at the lack of length to the clothing that Debbie and I wore, not to mention the newly blonde hair that I had carefully ironed for her on the condition that I could wear her sweater with my miniskirt, and the *Twiggy* (the latest Carnaby Street model of the pop culture) eyelashes I painted on below my eyelids to complement the heavy mascara and eyeshadow on top. I am

certain and grateful that this neighbor, a natural blonde with clear blue eyes that needed
no makeup to be beautiful, was praying for
us. It is likely one of the things that kept me
going without realizing it at the time that
this kind woman was offering silent yet fervent prayers.

From there, we headed on further down the
road to a home as chaotic and disheveled as
our German friends was neat and tidy. We
picked up the eldest member of the group, a
sturdy young man named Simon who daily
wore a chestnut colored velveteen corduroy
coat with a faux (long before anyone in the
States knew that word) sheepskin lining and
wingtip shoes of enormous size. Actually, *all*
wingtip shoes look enormous, regardless of
size, but his were *huge*. The space between
the hem of his pants and the vastness of his
shoes revealed lime green socks that had the
texture of fur. Simon had a lot of hair. A shock
of auburn that shot out in all directions, but
leaned mostly to one side at the part that
exposed flakes of dandruff. Large ones. I
am not sure if he was aware of it. Or that he
cared. He looked like a professor at seventeen from behind his thick black glasses and
rattled off complex thoughts with ease and
a style unique to anyone I had ever known.
He was obviously well read and went on to

become a journalist, and I imagine a very good one. He was a man amongst children in his own special and eccentric way.

His Mom was a jolly Bohemian lady who always had a ready smile and seemed wholly content where she was at any moment. On her days to drive, she careened up to our driveway since she routinely ran late, as we piled in and she tore off again, a delicious smile on her face filling out her features and offering no apologies. Wedged between Simon and his mother in the front seat sat his little cherubic faced brother, Mikey, whose milk sloshed wildly over the side of the bowl of Cheerios he would casually eat as we sped along. From my cramped position next to the rest of the youthful passengers in the back seat of the rusty old stationwagon, I could see the road whiz by underneath my feet through the hole in the floorboards.

And not unlike the little belts to secure a sanitary napkin, those were the days before seatbelts to secure little bodies in place! The thing that kept us all from being catapulted around within the speeding car was the fact that we were all compressed like sardines until we came to another screeching halt at the bus stop.

On a day when we arrived in time to catch our breath before the bus arrived, we got to listen to our final comrade, a tough girl named Denise with a big heart that she liked to disguise under heavy make up and revealing clothing that made my sister and I look like total amateurs. Her eyelashes were huge glue-ons from the dime store (another vintage concept since they are now called dollar or dollar plus stores) and her hair was bleached and ratted. She had a penchant for profanity and a cigarette going the entire wait. A *cigarette?!* I mean, she was *fifteen*, and on a school day?! If *I* was shocked, imagine the sweet and quiet German kids. My brother, Craig, just took it all in while Denise proceeded to regale us with drunken tales of being with twenty-something aged guys over the weekend, with raunchy, lurid details.

Simon just looked on in disgust, yet uncharacteristically reserving comment. When the bus finally pulled up, the driver, a tall, thin man named Mr. Dobbins whose large eyes peeked out from behind big, black framed glasses pulled open the bi-fold door as his Adam's apple bobbed in time with the movement and the creaking whoosh sound it made. He perused us all carefully, waiting patiently for the finale to Denise's monolog.

Simon cleared his throat and with a great

flourish, exclaimed: "*Congratulations, Trash-trap*! We have been standing here for three minutes and twenty-seven seconds and in that brief time, you have managed to utter *nine* profane words!" All of the rest of us leaned toward the open bus door yet froze. Denise looked at Simon as if she had noticed him for the first time, took a huge, long draw on her cigarette, and while blowing out the heavy stream of smoke in his direction, snarled, "Well, *f-you*, and make it *ten!*" as she dropped her still ignited butt on the road and stomped onto the school bus.

Now in that case, as the true story is retold, and a small slice of life is revealed, it seems like Denise had pretty darn good comedic timing, even if she wasn't attempting to be funny and a dramatic use of profanity *(at least in her rebuttal statement!)* And in his own way, I bet Simon had to tip his hat to her whenever he thought of that interchange. *Touché'!* And even if I leaned more toward Simon's opinion, I had to hand it to Denise and her ability to hold her own.

And what in the world does this memory have to do with my healing today? *Plenty*. Going backward to the places that injure and impact us allow for growth and recovery. *We have to feel to heal.*

A friend once told me that my husband, Gary, was romantically involved with Simon's little brother Mikey's wife (or was trying to be) when he was married to me and still drinking alcoholically. *Good heavens!* The last time I had seen Mikey, his little round face was bobbing up and down as he gnashed his Cheerios in the front seat of the rusty stationwagon! When had *he* gotten married? And when had I gotten so lonely and wounded that *my* need for attention and affection crossed healthy boundaries and I went looking for love in all of the wrong places as well? And how had that been an unconscious, un-discussed pattern modeled for me as I grew up?

Absurd as all of it sounds, in a nutshell, it is truly about forgiveness. *Forgiveness is the only antidote to insanity.* It is something we need to focus on every day of our lives until it becomes our way of being. None of us are immune for the need for it—for ourselves and others. Breathe in experience. Breathe out forgiveness. Make forgiveness a *decision*. Not a blind acceptance of injustice. Speak up. Speak out. Defend yourself and others. But when it is all said and done, forgive and let go. Surrender. *Your life depends on it.*

My time with Chasta has done more for me to unearth all of those frozen feelings than any other therapist ever could. She has taught me with her incredible horse wisdom and earthy smells and warm body to love the weird and wonderful humanity *in all of us*.

And two generations later, I still occasionally see the kind German woman walking her dog down that old stretch of road when I drive by, her hair still just as naturally blonde, though now platinum, and imagine that she is still praying for all of us — and grateful for it. I think of every soul* mentioned in this story and hope they know of the peace of which she prays. I have tasted it and would love to share my portion, knowing that by doing so will expand it.

W. H. Auden said it well: *"you shall love your crooked neighbor with your crooked heart."*

*Some names have been changed to protect privacy.

The view from the bus stop thirty eight years later.....

Chapter Seven

Collect to Connect:
Grow and Let Go

I caught the collecting bug from my Uncle Loren as a small child fascinated by his eye-popping array of antiques of every description. He had many categories that he was drawn to and the acquisition of one piece led to the next until he had groups of similar things displayed everywhere.

Most of what he sought was from the mid to late 1800s which was considered the golden age for what was a new era in manufacturing. The art of chromolithography decorated fanciful tin containers that graced private homes and country stores and included the fluted metal horns, shaped like a lily blossom and bedecked in rose patterned designs that amplified the sound from the first wax cylinder records of the early phonographs. Oh, how I loved to watch Loren crank the handle to start the mechanism that caused the cylinder to roll and the needle to move down and touch the record to hear a scratchy version of a rousing polka, a lilting waltz or the jolly *Barney Google with the Goo-Goo-Googly Eyes!*

Advertising of the period featured beautiful women wearing long flowing dresses and large flowered hats, rosy cheeked children and domestic animals, usually with an idyllic background of a lush country farm setting. To say that the jewel toned prints in ornate frames and the huge tin containers with curved compartments covered in flurid script lettering for various spices appealed to me would not be adequate---I was *mesmerized!* Being around lovely old things made my heart beat faster and it seemed to transport me to another place in time. The attraction was magnetic.

Loren had a huge collection of musical instruments with wax and metal records and all manner of arcade and commercial machines including player pianos and mechanical banjos. His intricately carved music boxes featured fanciful figural shapes under beveled glass that would strike brass bells in rhythm with the tunes, all predating electricity and were true mechanical wonders for children of all ages.

But what started it all for me was his paper ephemera collection, mostly advertising giveaways that were complimentary offerings from country stores when you purchased a tin of coffee or a box of biscuits. Again, the genre was what appealed to me deeply as a small child: mostly farm scenes with robust children, a peaceable kingdom of animals—often featuring the shaggy ponies of my dreams, frolicking with joyful abandon. Some were pressed and die-cut paper attached to calendars or a recipe booklet advertising baking powder, but most were called trade cards, which often ran in a series designed to keep the turn-of-the-century housewives coming back for more. Because of their ephemeral nature, most did not survive, much like the advertising supplements to newspapers today. (Let's hope, once read, that these papers are recycled properly!) But thankfully, the wondrous appeal of those old trade cards were appreciated by many and became the forerunner of today's scrapbooking craze since they were often glued into large albums to be enjoyed again and again on rainy days and were also made into personalized "calling cards" given away during social visits, known as "coming to call." These trade and calling cards and die-cut shaped images became known collectively as "scrap."

It was holding one of these large albums of color drenched scrap images that marked my beginning as a collector: a caretaker and steward of history. Every page had many cards and figural shapes, each more enchanting to me than the next. There were some loose ones between many of the pages and when Loren sensed my joy in perusing them, offered that I choose one to take home. *Oh!* Suddenly I was a kid in a candy store, but the booty was far sweeter! After much deliberation, comparing each delicate piece, going back and forth between children with ponies, puppies, goats, chickens and strutting roosters, I finally settled on one little girl with curly hair, die-cut to look like a paper doll, in a fancy dress holding a kitty that looked like my own *"Fluffy"* at home.

As I held it in my small hands, it seemed to me that I *knew* this girl and could truly understand how she felt to hold the prize of a soft and purring cat. My uncle cautioned me to take *very* good care of it, which I took to heart. It remains a treasure for me today and transports me back into the den of my favorite aunt and uncle's lovely old brick home where the leaded glass bookcases were filled with antique toys, high button boots and jeweled hat pins and their cookie jar filled with my Norwegian aunt's homemade perfection.

From the moment that I was taught my first history lesson at school, my fascination with other people, places and things began. Becoming a collecting buddy of my Uncle Loren at an early age, I learned much about where the items originated and why particular pieces were highly prized, including art glass designed by the Louis Comfort Tiffany Company of New York or handmade papier mâché candy containers shaped like wild rabbits that were created by family cottage industries in Bavaria.

As my ability to earn an income blossomed with regular neighborhood baby sitting jobs, so then did my opportunity to purchase my own treasures. This early magnetism to old objects became a fever to haunt any place where antiques may be found. This will really date me, but my generation of collectors knew a heyday that will never again be repeated. Loren was incredibly ahead of his time, amassing an *enormous* overall collection that filled museums when the vast majority of people at that time still thought of it as "old junk." Those were the days when second hand stores were filled with fantastic wonders and sold for next to nothing. We went to country barn sales, auctions and spent entire days in small towns full of numerous shops crowded with the gleanings of yesteryear.

There were also large shows to look forward to where dealers spent the year traversing America and often other continents to fill their booths with everything from huge architectural accoutrements like carved pillars and ornate stained glass windows to small and rare pieces of period estate jewelry.

Collecting treasures for most of my life, spending much of any disposable income and beyond on the things that I dearly loved, it was time to head for one of my favorite large shows in Portland, Oregon. Married and in my early thirties yet still childless, I entered the huge complex of buildings like a kid on an Easter hunt searching for the golden egg. By midmorning I had found a small straw-stuffed jointed Teddy bear with glass eyes from the early 1900s to add to my stash at home as well as a porcelain lidded jar that once housed toothpaste lauded by the Queen herself.

As I turned a corner, my heart skipped a beat as a very charming booth filled with all the things that most appealed to me beckoned. I smiled and greeted the proprietress as my gaze scanned her careful display. Filled with advertising memorabilia, wonderful time worn toys, lovely textiles, transferware ironstone dishes and other country primitives, I was *captivated* and soon began placing a few items to be purchased on the beautiful carved showcase that she used as a counter which supported an ornate 19th century brass and oak cash register to ring up sales.

Her tastes and choices were all the type of things I had and loved at home and when she was writing up a receipt for the pieced quilt of calico fabrics, and the German toy mohair horse with a velvet and leather saddle mounted on a wooden platform with wheels, it occurred to me that letting go of these treasures must be hard for her. "You have *such* lovely things!" I offered. "*How* can you part with them?!" Without hesitation, she smiled broadly. "It's *easy!* My son wants a new bicycle for Christmas and this is how I can provide it for him. I love old things and am sure that will not change, but my family *always* comes first."

It was in that moment when something shifted in me. Most of all, I wanted to have a family and share her values. I *did* love old treasures, and like her, probably always will. The quality and beauty fascinates me and I truly feel like a steward, a caretaking guardian of preserving history. But in that defining moment, I knew beyond any perspective that I had known before, that all of the merchandise in her space that was attractive to me were merely *things.*

When my son, Evan, was born, he was nursed and rocked in a beautiful carved American oak chair and slept in a swinging cast iron cradle draped with time softened old quilts. I feel deeply connected to those who came before us, those who originally owned these pieces, even though these heirlooms did not originate in either of our biological families. On the day Evan rode his very first bicycle, I thought of the lovely woman from Oregon and understood fully how very much a mother loves her son. It was not long after that when I sold my most rare German mohair jointed Teddy Bear with tin button eyes in order to purchase our first *real live* horse, Chad. He was the best investment I had ever made and left us with wonderful memories to last a lifetime.

Getting to know other collectors and dealers and the camaraderie we all enjoyed during those road trips before the days of Ebay was something very special—it allowed me to meet some of the greatest people that I have ever known. The collective antique malls of today simply cannot capture the spirit of the days when you made contact with each merchant personally and developed friendships where you could share stories about coming across a rare treasure like finding a needle in a haystack. The *things* were something we mutually enjoyed, but it was about the fact that they were hand-crafted and handed down by *people* that made them special.

But as wonderful as many of the dealers and collectors who I got to know were, like all good things, there was an underlying tendency for extremes. Some merchants and buyers became incredibly competitive amongst themselves and though the overall feeling of this fraternity was one of camaraderie, the darker human tendencies, based on individual insecurities, caused backstabbing and bickering which created ugly judgments and smugness, dividing the group into a large dysfunctional family.

As part of that subculture of people who became increasingly connected to one another, I personally experienced the tendency to have a love of old things become an addictive disorder. Though I was truly interested in being a healthy steward and caretaker of antiques, fascinated by the history, at the same time acquiring them became like some sort of feel good fix. We know that addictive patterns escalate over time and lead to wanting more while experiencing less satisfaction.

I knew other collectors and dealers who went over the top in their desire for more. It became a disease of accumulation. Beyond the need for an old chair to sit on or other practical, functional items, buying the next mint condition fascinating *thing* seemed to satisfy an inner hunger. *Temporarily.* And when we acquire *stuff,* when we are looking for love and acceptance, it can so easily become a vicious cycle, leading to behaviors that can run amok. Speaking from experience and observation, it got out of control and created debt and heartache for many. Some of those I knew acquired such numbers of material things that they filled every nook and cranny of their shops and homes, stacking them sideways and upside down in piles gone awry. It was sobering for me to discover that this inner hunger for love and connection could never be satisfied with just one more *thing* and how possessions can become burdensome taskmasters, taking our precious reserves of energy.

So today as a middle aged mother and adult child my collecting and acquiring days are over. There is a very big difference between feeling a sense of peaceful *connection to and appreciation for* lovely things and being *attached to* them in a hoarding, unhealthy manner. It is time for me to let go and pare down, a process that is well underway. And as much as I would love to meet and share with customers personally, I too, will continue to offer old treasures on my website since that has become the most convenient method for many. But I will always remember the glory days — the first time that I saw a six foot tall German goose feather Christmas tree adorned with three dimensional figural Dresden pressed paper ornaments and tin clips in the shape of birds which housed beeswax candles at a show in Gaithersburg, Maryland. Ironically, I was taken there by my wonderful cousin Brent, son of my Uncle Loren who had been my first mentor. Though it sat on a cold floor in a drafty barn building on a country fairgrounds, it felt as resplendent as the day when it graced a Victorian parlor and stood behind pocket doors, waiting to have the candles lit at the last moment and then revealed to the wide-eyed children of the holiday household. I could not financially afford the rare and valuable ornaments, much less the tree, but just to have seen it in person with my own eyes was thrill enough, indeed! Enjoying photos in a book or a display in a shop or museum does not require ownership and can be just as satisfying.

After passing on what is truly precious to the memories of our son, the rest will go back into circulation to the next group of history loving children like me who could care enough about a scrap of paper to keep it for fifty years. I have *more* than enough.

These days, I want to simplify my spaces and schedule to spend more time with my family and animals and serving others on our own little farm that resembles the scenes on those trade cards of long, long ago, *shaggy ponies and all.*

Advertising Trade Card circa 1880

For reprints of Connie's Vintage Ephemera
Collection, visit ███ constancefunk ████ @
and her Zazzle site at *gmail .con*
www.zazzle.com/ woodylanefarm
www. woodylanefarm. com

Chapter Eight

Warts and All

One of the most special souls that I have ever had the pleasure to call my friend was a man known to many as "Big George." As you might imagine, this nickname came to be because of his large physical stature and wide girth, but to me, it represented the size of his heart, which was enormous.

I started buying antiques from George when still a teenager wearing miniskirts and long hair parted down the middle, a ghastly combination to me now in retrospect. Though I was young in age, I connected with George as an 'old soul' since we shared a mutual passion for the history and craftsmanship that went into creating handmade beauty. He had a great depth of knowledge about life and the way things work that had far more to do with being tuned into his intuitive guidance than it did time spent in a classroom.

George could fix anything that was broken

and created incredible beauty from what someone else may see as a castoff. He had gigantic hands that in no way appeared to be instruments of finesse, yet they were so tuned into his inner knowing as well, and capable of the most delicate manipulations.

Once I brought him an antique folk art carved wooden cart that went with a lovely horse that used to be part of an apple tree. The wheels were lined with hand cut tin and each spoke carved by hand. Two of the original spokes were missing, likely after years of play by a young child who had been gifted with this charming toy by a loving adult. After leaving the rare piece with George for repairs, when I returned for it, I honestly could not tell which ones had been replaced. George *loved* that.

His workshop looked like a bomb had exploded in the center of it all. Workbenches were strewn with tools, half-finished projects lay on their sides and there was nothing that resembled an aisle or path---just obstacles everywhere. Yet everything there was fascinating in that George saw the hidden potential and knew that he could restore something that was long forgotten into its former loveliness from a curvaceous armoire to a fanciful carousel horse. He restored a charming small carved horse from an 1890's carousel from New York for me that looks *just* like a miniature version of Chasta years before she came into my life. And his new creations were always carved out of old wood and appeared to be vintage entirely. He carved beautiful duck, swan and goose decoys and replicated items from famous museums, adding his own special signature touches that made them so unique. As I watch the wild Canadian geese that claim our pond as their summer home, I think of George's creations in all of their graceful poses and the vivid imagination that could see the lovely forms in a block of old wood and bring them to life in three dimensions and give them the worn patina that suggested the softness of time.

George's personal appearance was usually as disheveled as the state of his shop. It was just not a high priority with him though seeking and sharing beauty definitely was. You could usually count on seeing him in the same old denim bib overalls yet when gifted with a jaunty wool tweed cap brought from England by his closest friends in the antiques business, he rarely went without it and loved to share how he came to sport it whenever complimented.

George and I maintained a close friendship over many years of buying and selling antiques together and loved to compare found treasures. As we shared our passion for beautiful old things, we also felt comfortable talking with each other about the joys and trials of our personal lives. He was protective in a fatherly sort of way and always reminded me that I deserved the best and was quick to encourage whenever I needed support, calling me by the formal version of my name, *Constance*, something I seldom hear but always feels endearing. One day when I was feeling blue, he reminded me that he would *always* love me, *"Warts and all."*

We met weekly for a meal at a local eatery called Kate's Café and took advantage of the two-for-one salad bar offered on Wednesdays. I would come in on my lunch hour with my dental office staff and they would occupy their own table while I sat in the back with George to catch up on what great old treasure one of us may have stumbled across.

George often handled the sales of local personal property estates, selling off the entire contents of households from the furniture to the Tupperware. Some had a nice selection of antiques and collectibles, which was his forte, but he was willing to handle it all---a great service for people needing to liquidate.

He was in the process of pricing and selling an estate and felt that he had been able to give the owner a good assessment of the estimated total worth when by complete surprise found the greatest and most valuable treasure of all downstairs in the damp cellar in a shoebox next to the old Mason jars full of spiders. The box had some string and a few odds and ends and also a rare manifestation of a piece of history of our nation and world.

George looked like the cat that ate the canary the entire time we heaped our plates with the bountiful selection from the salad bar. Once seated at our table covered in gold and white checkered oilcloth, he began to tell me about getting to the end of pricing the household items and finding the treasure hidden in the cellar with no record of its origins.

Clasped in his oversized hands roughened by years of labor, he smiled a radiant grin that exposed his need for dental work as he opened my hands and rolled the items into them and then closed my fingers into a grasp as he whispered, *"only you will appreciate these like I do."*

Heavy for their size and cool to the touch were a matched pair of silver cloak hooks that belonged on an early American fireplace. They had raised glass domes that housed handmade artisan reverse on glass etched decorations. I had to hold them up to the light in the back of the old café to see the design that I knew was sacred because I could feel it tingling into my hands and by the tender expression on George's time etched face.

Each depicted a black man, naked but for torn breeches, shackled and chained to the ground looking toward the Heavens and beseeching in the printed words surrounding the rim, *"Am I not a man, am I not your brother?"*

Tears of deep compassion filled my eyes as I stared at the works of art that revealed such tragedy. I felt George's meaty hands cover mine and looked up to see his own tears rolling down into hair on his face that had more to do with not wanting to shave than a beard. We just sat there silently except for my snuffling and the background noise of the lunch crowd for what seemed like a long time before he spoke.

"I did some research on these," George offered. "They are rare artisan pieces created for the Abolitionist movement that were sold to wealthy Northern supporters of the Underground Railroad to free slaves."

"Incredible," was all I could whisper. "How in the world did they end up here in the Pacific Northwest down in an old cellar inside a box that most people would have tossed?!"

"No one knows," he replied, but had already sold them to a seasoned collector from San Francisco for top dollar and able to turn the money over to his client, who frankly would never have known this windfall had it not been for the honesty and integrity of George.

That moment in time is indelibly recorded in my heart, with George as my brother as well as the artist, the sympathizer that purchased them and the pleading black man who was depicted and likely separated from the family he loved. Brothers and sisters all are we.

The collective consciousness has recorded the brutality of that time in history in all of us and we as a human family continue to have much forgiveness work to do. Eckhart Tolle describes the collective "pain-body" in his remarkable book, *A New Earth, Awakening* to *Your Life's Purpose*. He states: *"The pain-body, however is not just individual in nature. It also partakes of the pain suffered by countless humans throughout the history of humanity, which is a history of continuous tribal warfare, of enslavement, pillage, rape, torture and other forms of violence. The pain still lives in the collective psyche and is being added to on a daily basis, as you can verify when you watch the news tonight or look at the drama in peoples' relationships."*

Mr. Tolle goes on to say: *"In fact, the suffering inflicted on Native and Black Americans has not been confined to those two races, but has become part of the collective American pain-body. It is always the case that both victim and perpetrator suffer the consequences of any acts of violence, oppression, or brutality. For what you do to others, you do to yourself."* And this brutality is not limited to man's inhumanity to man, but to what man has done to injure the plant and animal kingdoms. We must hold ourselves accountable each day and move toward respect for both our interconnectedness and mutual dependency. Mankind needs to take a good, long look in the mirror and see what is reflecting back.

Each day I ask for forgiveness and offer it out in my prayers for transgressions old and new. Those which I am personally responsible for and healing prayers for those of my ancestors. Forgive us our trespasses as we forgive those who trespass against us. Do unto others as you would have others do unto you. For certainly what Eckhart Tolle states about "what you do to others, you do to yourself" can be seen in a positive light as well, for the better we treat others, the more we nourish ourselves and vice versa. *Love thy neighbor as thyself and love thyself as thy neighbor.*

One day I got a call that George's enormous heart had given out. His death came as a huge shock for me since my beloved Uncle Loren who had sparked and encouraged my lifelong interest in old treasures and had been my first antiques mentor had also recently passed on ---each of them far too young and both immediately from heart attacks---I was reeling with grief thinking that these two men would have been as big a part of my son Evan's young life as they had been in mine.

I went to George's funeral with my close friend Jack, another local legend in the antiques world and my collecting buddy of many years. Jack had looked up to George as a big brother and they were trusted friends. Jack told me that he had lost his greatest mentor and first teacher in the business. We sat halfway back in the packed house and I closed my eyes as I listened to a gentleman who I recognized as an employee of one of the local post offices sing a familiar and comforting hymn. His voice was spectacular and soothing and it made me realize we know so little about the gifts people are given when we see them out of the context that we think we know. I wondered how many assembled there truly knew of the extent of the gift of God that was George. Whether they looked deeply beneath the bib overalls to that tender heart.

Powerful sadness for my losses welled deep in me and I began to weep. As the talented soloist's voice caressed the melody, I saw a clear moving picture behind my closed eyes, like an old reel to reel movie flitting across a screen. It was George, in his early youth in the Midwest, running through an open field with bare arms outstretched under faded denim overalls. His smiling face was surrounded by radiant light. Though it filled me with peace, I continued to cry, now in gratitude for the immense affection that I felt was mutual. Then I felt Jack's hand covering mine, much as George's had on that touching day in Kate's Café, as he reassured me in a whisper, "He is *free* now, Connie----he is running free" as if he could see what I was experiencing by reading my mind and heart without spoken words.

Within a year, a young and vital Jack has passed on to join them. Three very unique men with large and tender hearts had them stop beating suddenly and far too early in their fourth, fifth and sixth decades of life.

Life is precious. Learn from each other. Support and encourage each other's dreams. Share the joys of being alive. George Eliot captured this essence when she said, *"What do we live for if it is not to make life less difficult for each other?"*

Thank you, George. And Loren. And Jack. And *Chasta*. For loving me, *warts and all.*

Depiction of slaves on Colonial bed curtains, created for the Abolitionist movement supporters. Courtesy of the Marion and Theresa Hilton collection.

Chapter Nine

A Boy and his Dog

The Yogi is in...

"I want a Golden Retriever" my husband Gary announced totally out of the blue in the sixth year of our marriage. We are both animal lovers and had two cats at the time and it struck me as odd that we had never discussed getting a dog before this mention. "Is that what you had growing up?" I answered with a question.

"No," he said quietly, hardly audible, "I never *had* a dog." "What do you mean---? *Every-*

one has a dog!" I replied in surprise. "I just never had a dog and always wished for one" he said with a faraway look in his eyes that were cast downward. *"Wow!"* I thought my heart would break for my sensitive spouse who had surprised me with female sister cats as a gift to keep me company while I was in college. "Why a Golden Retriever?" I asked. "I have just always admired them ... I even have a name picked out for the one I want— *Yogi."*

We did not have a fenced yard at our first home at that time but the patio area was enclosed and due to the heartfelt expression by Gary, I did not hesitate and started looking for breeders immediately. God knows our hearts and needs before we do and that weekend there was a festival in the little waterfront town near where we lived that had vendors out to take advantage of the crowds coming to jig for smelt, a type of small fish that navigates the waters of the channel that the community is built around.

Sandwiched between the service club barbeque stand and the T-shirt tables was a young man with several golden retriever puppies for sale that had just been weaned from their mother. The proud Papa, a handsome, muscular animal with the characteristic square head of the male and wide set brown eyes sat next to his pups with a slowly sweeping tail that was as much a wag as it was a protective gesture as he admired his progeny.

Before I had time to think, one of the puppies jumped up and looked intently at me with incredibly soulful eyes and it was clear that he was the perfect gift for my tender hearted husband. Happy that the gentleman would take a check, I walked down the street to an interior design store that belonged to good friends and purchased a rag rug and a basket for transport. Needing to finish some business in town, the owner said that he would take the puppy home and I could pick him up later ----that way his mother could say goodbye and I could meet her. Purchasing a yellow ribbon from a nearby flower vendor, I tied it on him in a bow to symbolize his homecoming and kissed him on the nose. When it was time for me to return, I followed the directions to his home and there they were. The pup that I had chosen jumped up to greet me again and gave me that sweet yet serious expression that renewed my feeling that I had made the right choice, the yellow ribbon chewed soggy and bedraggled by his siblings still sweetly symbolic.

Promising Maggie, his pretty and doting mother, that he would be loved and taken good care of, I placed him gently in the basket and turned for the gate. Maggie gave me a sad but resigned and trusting look through large brown eyes as I stroked her neck and felt a terrible tug on my heart as we walked away. Before I could start the car, the tiny pup gave an ear piercing, heart wrenching wail and I took a deep breath. *"Hey, little one,"* I soothed. "we're on our way home and you will like it there." He wailed all the way, somewhere between a kitten's plaintive mew and a lamb's throaty baaa.

Stopping the car at home, he seemed to shift his awareness, something that my petting and coos had not accomplished. I lifted the basket and looked at the quivering form, wondering if I had made a good decision. Gary was resting on the bed, reading by the table lamp in an otherwise darkened room. I held the basket high so that he could not see his gift and told him that I had a surprise for him---he sat up with a questioning look as I tipped it over and plopped the fuzzy treasure down on the antique quilt bedspread. The look on Gary's face is one that I will always remember. The small boy inside the young man was revealed as he grinned from ear to ear. The puppy sniffed his hand as his rump gyrated furiously. "It's *Yogi*," Gary smiled, in a whisper, eyes filling with tears. He scooped up the puppy that he had always wanted like they were long lost friends. The lump in my throat told me that our lives would never be the same.

From that moment, they were inseparable. Gary took Yogi to work, on fishing trips and he was sure that he was the star of the dog obedience classes that we took him to. In short, they were best friends. Often when I was looking for Gary, I would find him on the floor nestled against his dog, one arm over the furry golden form who was now nearly as big as his human when stretched out in rest.

Those were very tough and tender years as Gary rode the roller coaster called active alcoholism and there were many times when only God and Yogi could offer him the unconditional love that every living being needs and deserves. Gary's secrets and his heart were safe with his dog and their bond was one of fierce loyalty and tenderness.

I was crazy about Yogi, too, and he helped our house feel like a home and our often struggling marriage feel like we were becoming a family. He regularly jumped up and knocked the gate handle loose and ran down a number of blocks to the office where I practiced dental hygiene, and waiting for a patient to open and enter the front door, would run in and sprint down the hall to my operatory where he would bump my elbow with his nose as I leaned over an unsuspecting patient.

A wonderful retired gentleman in my practice who was well known as a practical joker teased me about my constant ravings of the superior intelligence, remarkable behavior, and general handsomeness of my dog. We bantered back and forth as to who possessed the greater canine during every check-up appointment, sharing every clever story about our animal companions.

One day during his regular check-up exam, I left the operatory to develop a set of X-rays. Making a detour to a room where Yogi was waiting, I quickly put a white lab coat over his front legs and buttoned it up under his belly. The next step was to put on a pair of safety glasses over his eyes, resting them on his snout followed by a set of magnifying loops over his head in a wide silver band while he carefully allowed me to finish the job with a mouth mirror taped to the paw that he loved to "shake hands" with! I gave him a good scratch on the ruff and whispered *"Good dog!"* in his ear and had one of my co-workers wait with him until the time came for his appearance.

Returning to my operatory with the X-rays in hand, I casually asked my patient if he would consider being examined by a dental student in training from the university as a part of his internship. *"Absolutely!"* replied this retired gentleman who had his own collection of college degrees without hesitation.

On cue, in came Yogi and as I stepped back, he walked directly to my patient as if we had rehearsed it and foisted the paw in the air that held the mouth mirror! Taken aback, my patient turned in the direction of this furry form, whose tail under the lab coat was swishing back and forth, the loops now a wee bit askew with his paw on his arm and let out an unrestrained belly laugh. *"Well done!"* he acquiesced.

When Evan was born, the nurse who taught our delivery classes told us to take the cotton hat that they had put on Evan's head to retain his body heat when he arrived into the world and tie it to Yogi's collar so that he would be familiar with the scent and recognize it when Evan came home so that he would accept and protect him. *And that he did.* We have a wonderful photo of Yogi greeting Evan with a careful sniffing as an infant for the first time, the cotton hat tied to his collar, reminding him of his precious charge.

At fourteen, Yogi was showing signs of his advancing age when we moved to the country so that we could realize our dream of having horses. He loved the open space but lacked his former energy to romp and his zest for life. He spent a lot of time resting in various places on the acreage under the canopy of trees until he hardly moved at all. Yogi's final diagnosis by our caring vet was renal failure and he advised us that the kindest thing that we could do would be to end his suffering.

It did not seem possible that this dog who had been with us through sickness and health, richer or poorer and all the rest would ever leave us. The dog who had survived skunks and porcupines and dressed up for Halloween with our son, Evan. Our first dog. Our *Yogi.*

Gary was so devastated with sadness that he had to leave the vet's operatory while Yogi was still alive and took Evan to wait in the car. I shared with them that Yogi had died without pain peacefully in my arms, as I reminded him over and over what a good dog he had been to us and how much we all loved him. Three year old Evan cuddled up to his father and stroked him tenderly as if he was petting Yogi while Gary choked on his tears all the way as I drove them carefully home.

A few weeks later, I returned to the vet's office to pick up Yogi's ashes from the cremation and we took them outside for a ceremony to celebrate the life of a dog we had all loved so dearly.

As we gathered outside for our final goodbyes, a reluctant Gary took a long deliberate breath as I said that as hard as funerals are, they are a time to celebrate life with joy as well as sadness. "This is a *funeral?!*" Evan asked, looking startled. "Well, *Yes,*" I answered, and was starting to explain when he turned to run toward the house. *"I'll be right back!"* he hollered over his shoulder. Gary looked at me with a deep sigh and a weak smile and sat down on a garden bench and lowered his head onto his outstretched legs.

Evan emerged down the porch steps wearing a black cape and top hat that had been his magician's costume for Halloween over his striped shirt, a solemn look on his face as he announced in a deep measured voice---"I am the *under*taker." Never surprised but always amazed at Evan's ability to make connections, I said "I *see.*" To which he replied, "Just like the one in Oliver Twist." Then it clicked. We had taken him to see a stage play of the beloved Dickens tale when he was only two years old and he was totally captivated by every moment from our front row seats. Astonishing.

Evan held the urn of ashes in his arm and ceremoniously lifted the lid. We had agreed that each of us would sprinkle some of Yogi's ashes in his favorite places on our new little farm, where we planned to build a barn and get a horse, a lifelong dream. Gary and I each took a handful and tearfully tossed them in spots where we could picture him still as there, believing that his spirit would always be with us. Then Evan, a pre-schooler, gave us a comforting gaze and strode purposefuly with a faraway look in his eyes as he moved confidently from place to place sprinkling handfuls in relaxed abandon until we heard his voice softly singing. With each word, he increased the volume until we could hear the beautiful lyrics to the melo-

dy of the wondrous song from Disney's *The Lion King™* called *The Circle of Life*. Written and recorded by Elton John, the poignant lyrics helped a small boy make sense of his first true loss of a constant companion and his parents enormous grief. He *got it.*

A puppy that is long wished for is born, nurtured and then mourned by his mother when humans come to take him. The unbreakable bond of a boy and his dog times two generations. A three year old child. Parents and their son. Connect the dots. Sharing the joys of canine loyalty and the pain of goodbyes. Dust to dust.

The circle of life.

Father-Son-Puppy-Dog-Love

PART II

Trail Travel
The Best Way Out
is Through

Chapter Ten

Home Sweet Home

I absolutely *love* the game of baseball. My most favorite play is a dramatically close moment at the plate when the runner is called *safe at home* by an umpire who loves the game like I do and gets the chance to show it with a whooping holler to accompany his decisive hand gestures. He gets to call it like he sees it, which is no easy task to remain that fully present as not to conflict with the instant replay that is part of today's game. It thrills me to see the players pour out of the dugout as if they are liquid to high five the runner, especially if the run is the game winner. There is something remarkably symbolic that the game of baseball is so iconic in our culture and that coming home is what it is all about. Wes Westun, a professional baseball manager, described it well: *"Baseball is like church. Many attend, but few understand."*

An athlete playing baseball at any level will tell you there is a sweet spot where ball meets bat for maximum launch. And if you have spent any time in the stands, you can see it, hear it, even *feel* it in your own spectator sweet spot when a player makes that kind of connection. Then it's time to smile, sit back and watch the ball hit the bleachers in the outfield as the fans rush to catch a prize. It is delightful and fascinating to me to think that the beloved author, Robert Frost, penned these words: *"Nothing flatters me more than to have it assumed that I could write prose---unless it be to have it assumed that I once pitched a baseball with distinction."*

Golfers know it and watching those at the top of the game make it look easy to find, but they will tell you it remains elusive since it only happens a certain percentage of swings. The best batters in baseball of both genders only get a hit one third of the time. And what is happening in terms of physics? How much of it is a mental focus and seeing and believing that it is possible? Scientists tell us that it counts for plenty. Albert Einstein himself wrote: *"Imagination is everything. It is the preview of life's coming attractions."*

Musicians find the sweet spot when they become more than the sum total of the individual parts when they sing in four part harmony or an entire symphony swells in synchronicity. The leaders in the form of conductors and principal players facilitate the group flow. Again, the audience is able to participate fully on the receiving end as well since the melodies can transport them completely to another realm as they support what is happening onstage with their pleasure and appreciation.

So it is important to visualize an outcome and be able to use all of the senses to create the result you desire. Working and playing with horses is a lifetime journey of development and the sweet spot becomes a familiar phenomenon in so many ways. When the human and the horse have the ultimate connection—where there is understanding—a mutual goal—they will have relaxation and comfort even in the most difficult athletic maneuvers. Watch a master horseman like Pat Parelli or Mark Rashid move cows on horseback and it is as beautiful as any ballet and choreographed to a silent symphony that they have ears to hear which is understood instinctively by horse and cattle.

And yet the learning curve is often so steep with horses and with life that it is important not to be *attached* to an outcome. When harmony is lost, and horse and rider disconnect, it is time for a deep breath and a smile, *notic-*

ing. It is never the right time to berate yourself or your equine partner. Better to become aware of the rhythm of your breath and resume the dance again. Maybe more slowly. Perhaps just a few baby steps until that silent music that animates us all is heard again. Or wrap it up for the day and start over tomorrow, grateful for the experience.

A teacher and author who I admire greatly, Tessa Bielecki, says it is "the bounce that counts" as we find our way — our resiliency to continue to seek and learn and grow. She has produced a series called *Wild at Heart, Radical Teachings of the Christian Mystics,* which I found to be fascinating. In fact, she feels the essence of Christian Mysticism is *persevering forward movement.* And if you summed up the reason that the species Equus has survived so remarkably throughout the ages into three words, they would also be: *persevering forward movement.* Another quote by the brilliant Albert Einstein comes to mind: *"The most beautiful thing that we can experience is the mysterious. It is the source of all true art and science."* And it is in that place that bridges intellect and instinct that the sweet spot resides. Tessa is actively involved in Buddhist-Christian dialogue and has created *The Desert Foundation* to seek understanding and peace for all. She speaks of

Holy Daring as the way of the mystic and of *Disciplined Wildness* in redefining prayer. She cites Saint Teresa's *Holy Daring* as the ability to completely embrace everything that arises in your life.

Several spring seasons ago, I took our beautiful Arabian horse, Ritzy, to join Jonathan Field's Quilchena Ranch workshop in British Columbia, Canada. Jonathan is an incredibly accomplished horseman who communicates with horses in ways that build and develop that beautiful connection between horse and human where everything is soft and fluid and the rider's center of gravity moves with the horse's center to remain in a flow of movement that is natural and unimpeded. Fredric Pignon, the phenomenal Equine Artistic Director of *Cavalia*, a spectacular touring performance of horses and humans, says that since the music each night is live and the horses and musicians, riders and dancers are all considered equals, that each performance is absolutely unique. They have choreographed and practiced each piece in advance, but allow for the artistic expression of all participants and place a value there. The result is *astounding* and better than magic, for it is a *real* and fully sensory experience for all those fortunate to participate. The electric energy of the audience is serving the performers, human and equine, and vice versa.

Ritzy and I were scheduled to be gone for a week in Canada, and usually I could become mildly to acutely homesick fairly easily not long after my departure. In fact, in the past, I could create the anxiety of homesickness in my mind that would translate to my cells and give me a terrible tummy ache as I was *packing my bags!* But this time with Ritzy on the mountain trails gave me such a profound focused connection that we found our sweet spots together in a rushing stream, crossing a bridge, or just stopping to rest and relax together in the shade of an old tree by the creek.

Horses instinctively know this sweet spot of contentment when they are in a focused yet neutral grazing mode, or half asleep in the sun, switching their tails to keep the flies away, or in the perfect synchronicity of the entire herd moving as one. As human part-ners, we need to help them find and recog-nize their sweet spots of relaxation and con-nection when they are with *us.*

Halfway through the week, I was laying in the grass eating a sandwich on a perfect spring day as Ritzy munched the tender green sprouts next to me when I had a realization that the old familiar pang of homesickness had not made its presence known. *At all.* I was so absorbed in our connection and the gentle breeze that soothed us that my *complete ease* is what felt natural. I was totally comfortable in my own skin. I looked over at dear old Ritz, scratched his leg and realized that he was, too, an ear bending toward me, his eye liquid soft. On the final day, I was ready to make the trip home, but not *aching* to be there. Just profoundly grateful to be where I was.

Though I had understood the expression *Home Is Where the Heart Is* on an intellectual and philosophical level, this was an experiential epiphany in my body as well. My connection to my self, God and all of life got bigger that week, thanks to my friends, that incredibly sacred land, and mostly to an aging sorrel chestnut horse who knew what this trip meant to me on a very personal level. Though he would look longingly back at the lush grass below in his paddock on the long ascent up the mountain in the morning, his willing spirit overcame his personal desires and he offered the connection I craved, and then basked in the attention and affection of my enjoyment.

Tom Dorrance, a quiet rancher who understood horses beyond what most humans can comprehend and quietly influenced the natural horsemanship movement until his death, knew of the sweet spot intimately. He realized that it is not a place or a thing. It fills me with peace when I picture myself on a bench by our pond next to an open fire with my husband, son and animals all around me as we watch the ducks glide by and all tension drains away. As much as we love the comforts of our own personal spaces and the memories of those spaces can help you to feel safe, ultimately it is an inside job. And once you find it, your umbilical cord to all of life, you can take it with you. God Almighty is portable. The nomadic and legendary Lakota Medicine Man, Black Elk, shared the wisdom of these words: *"The Holy Land is everywhere."*

That's when you'll look up, shake off the dust and realize that you slipped under the tag, *safe at home.*

Black Elk by Craig Bartlett

Chapter Eleven

Let Nature Take Its Course

Nature's intrinsic ability to heal is beyond complete comprehension. Raising plants and animals on our small farm has given us so many remarkable examples of watching 'nature take its course' over the years.

I walk to my parents' home down our country road in the evenings to help them with dinner and personal care since they require help for their declining health. We are also blessed with devoted caregivers to assist our family and this ever increasing need in our society is a sacred duty that must be developed and nurtured if we are to collectively care for our elders in a global community.

As I cut through one of our pastures to get to the winding road, I noticed a couple out walking that I did not recognize who stopped me to say they had just seen a duck get hit by a car on the corner as they approached it. Looking to where they were pointing, I saw our ducks, George and Frank, scurrying up the bank, heading back toward the pasture. My neighbor, Nonie, who had seen the commotion, came out to offer support and had called a friend that lives nearby who is an expert on birds to come take a look at the situation. We watched the injured duck, George, as he struggled to move and would take a few staggering steps and collapse again, dragging the useless appendage behind while Frank followed, scurrying in frantic circles in an attempt to guide him from behind.

George's webbed foot appeared to be totally flattened like something out of the old Warner Brothers™ cartoon when Wile E. Coyote would get run over yet again by a Mack truck or freight train in pursuit of the Roadrunner and go from three dimensions to a complete pancake. In the next scene, he is back again, as if brand new and even more determined. Sadly, not so with George who continued to collapse in a heap and then get up and drag his crushed leg and foot.

When the bird expert friend arrived shortly after, he encouraged the ducks down to the pond and this helped Frank to calm down and focus on driving George to the water's edge where they both entered the summer stillness of the surface---Frank seamlessly and George in a painful splash. "All you can do now is to let nature take its course" was the advice of a man who has lived in the rhythm of the seasons all of his life, keeping domestic animals and surrounded by wild ones.

Daily I kept grain scattered close to the pond where Frank kept a careful watch over George while he paddled in jerky movements with the injured leg and foot dangling in the water like an unwelcome rudder. I also noticed that he hobbled up the bank and rested for long periods in the shade under the stone benches, realizing that his handicap increased his vulnerability as a "dead duck."

A few weeks passed and one day I noticed the injured leg was no longer being drug on land or in the water, but bent backwards and held up on his body near his tail feathers in what appeared to be comfortable rest. On land, it required George to hop around to get grain but his one-legged balance had become remarkable and he was learning to swim with a solo webbed foot with amazing directional accuracy as well, nearly keeping up with his best buddy and nursemaid, Frank.

Almost imperceptibly, George was restored to what appeared to be full commission, and in fact, experts tell us that which is healed from brokenness is often stronger for it. And this phenomenon is not limited to the physical body but to the mind and spirit as well.

Once again, I believe this story illustrates what we can learn from the animal kingdom and how God has designed the capacity to heal into every creature. The unique difference with animals, especially animals in their wild and natural habitat is that they do not often fight against or put energy into resisting the pain or discomfort or inconvenience of an injury or an illness. They do not berate themselves for allowing it to happen or blame and resent someone else for causing it. Because they readily achieve acceptance of the situation of *what is*, the flow of the rhythms of the complex processes of the immune system are undisturbed and able to achieve maximum function. George could have given in to a vicious circle of pain and fear over his injury and exhausted himself which would have overridden his natural ability to heal. Instead, he adapted by surrendering to the injury, putting his energy into the *solution* of healing by resting himself in protected areas for long periods and no doubt was strengthened by the water therapy of his pond a little at a time, responding to his greatest instinct. It is all about acceptance rather than resistance.

I was gifted with a wonderful book (ironically given to me by my Watsu water therapist Liz Bart!) called *Radical Acceptance: Living Life with the Art of a Buddha* by Tara Brach, Ph. D. The author writes in the prologue to this poignant and practical guide, "*Radical acceptance reverses our habit of living at war with experiences that are unfamiliar, frightening or intense. It is the necessary antidote to years of neglecting ourselves, years of judging and treating ourselves harshly, years of rejecting this moments experience. Radical acceptance is the willingness to accept ourselves and our life as it is. A moment of Radical Acceptance is a moment of genuine freedom.*" Tara Brach's concept of *Radical Acceptance* sounds very much like Christian Saint Teresa's *Holy Daring.* We are all One.

George the duck symbolized a radical acceptance of his injury but took steps, wobbling on one leg, each day to heal it. As I observed his progress, he appeared to be wholly content and focused on looking for insects or serenely gliding across the pond, even if he had to make more effort to navigate.

And as humans, our emotional illnesses and injuries often cripple us more than the physical ones and now science clearly understands the interconnection between them as inseparable.

But by contrast, due to her experiences in domesticity at the hands of humans Chasta came to me with an incredible amount of what is known by equine behaviorists as "opposition reflex." Basically translated, she usually did the opposite of what I requested. *She resisted.* Often mightily. Master horseman, author and clinician Chris Irwin says that there are three kinds of horses: "Yes horses, No horses and Maybe horses." Though she sometimes said "Maybe" in the beginning, Chasta also frequently and clearly said "No" and often *"Absolutely not!"* And master horseman Pat Parelli reminds me that if my horse says, "No!" it is because I am asking the question wrong or I am asking the wrong question. And Heaven knows that I am trying to get it right!

Though Chasta is *always* entitled to her opinion about any given situation, I do not believe that it is her inherent nature to be obstinate — she basically has a sweet and quiet--- though very alert--- disposition, yet she can also be fiercely independent. I feel that many of her experiences before coming to me caused her not to trust people and I continued to unwittingly contribute to that pattern with my frequent ineptitude as I committed to learning all I could about interspecies communication and partnering with Equine in a mutually healthy way. *Chasta thought she needed to resist to survive.*

And, in fact, her resistance is encoded in her DNA. One of the most fascinating and valuable books about horses and healing that I have read is called: *Tuning In: Equine Cranio-Sacral Therapy and Somato-Emotional Release* by E. Bailey Tune, LMT, CST. She explains eloquently how animals, including humans, live by instinct where survival depends on defensive physical self protection in the form of resistance. The evidence of her own remarkable personal balance between intellect and instinct has created a book that reads like poetry and resonates with truth. So much that the first time that I opened my copy and began to read the overview and principles aloud to my horses while sitting on a mounting block in the pasture just before sunset, something truly amazing occurred. My understanding on an intuitive level and deep relationship with the resonance of the truth of the words caused a spontaneous unwinding of and release of torqued connective tissue at a cellular level within me and the horses. One hand was resting on the jowl of Gaela, the other held the book and Chasta was standing nearby. I could observe and feel the collective shift that happened for all of us, especially Gaela, who had a physical connection, and the most powerful response and release. I am a believer and *highly* recommend this work, pioneered by Bailey and her colleagues.

I believe that Chasta entered my world to help me to see that she was mirroring this pattern of resistance in my own life. Too often I was struggling to accept the *parts of my life that I could not change or control*---which, if you are a caring person, is a significant amount of external circumstances. I could make myself sick with worry over the state of the environment, politics that I did not understand or agree with, women and children and animals being mistreated, and the list goes on. Today, I am far more practiced in living in the present moment in acceptance---not of abuse and greed---but of that which animates the life in all and that solutions lie in the stillness of prayer and positive actions.

Chasta has been a very steep learning curve for me as a teacher because of her need to

have me be so aware, so sensitive and effective and provocative. She rarely cuts me
much slack and always expects my personal
best. She is a tough customer because I believe that she is supremely aware of my deep
desire to be her trusted leader and she wants
me to *earn it,* knowing in the long run it will
mean more to both of us. The old-fashioned
way, by the sweat of my brow and the ex-
pansion of my heart which creates lightness
of touch. And the ability to find the softness
from deep within.

Once in our early days together, Chasta and
I accompanied friends on a trail ride to a
sandy beach along the channel near where
we live and since our previous ride which
had been lovely and invigorating until it included a dangerous bolt, I chose to take advantage of the wide sandy trails to practice
our *ground skills* and build our partnership
by leading her from behind, changing directions and walking and trotting to practice our
transitions. I sent my friends along ahead on
horseback and Chasta and I were doing really well until there was a rise and my friends
and their horses disappeared over the crest
of the hill. Realizing that her herd had gone
ahead without us, fear of separation was ignited within her and Chasta whinnied shrilly
and it became my job to become her trusted

leader. Actually, it had been my job all along but I had flunked because she was pulling on the line to surge ahead and join them.

Helping her to become accepting of and confident of *my* leadership, I asked her to move sideways in the deep sand and she did, though her head was turned sharply, searching for her four legged friends. To change her pattern, I suggested that she go sideways in the other direction and though her body moved that way, her head turned wildly again to locate her equine brethren. Though going through the motions of doing what I was requesting, she was totally distracted and moving in her reactive right brain. We needed to merge our minds and hearts and spirits as well as our bodies by gaining emotional connection. So I upped the ante by driving her sideways at the trot, not easy for either of us to navigate in the deep sand. But Chasta had so much magnetic energy to the other horses that she trotted sideways like a circus pony or elegant equine dressage queen ---the momentum was incredible—I could hardly go fast enough! Yet I was no longer guiding her in any real way---she was just a rhythmically moving force. Horses can be so amazingly athletic when they are properly motivated, and in this case, sadly, mostly about fear of abandonment, even though the person who most wanted to help her was just on the other side.

At some point, we were both tired on every level and I wished that I had emptied my bladder beforehand, but I felt determined to support her need to feel safe with me as her leader so I kept it up. *Then I felt it!* A definite shift. Her switch tripped from right brained reactive fear which created the opposition to a left brained acceptance which created softness. In that moment, I felt as if we were floating in slow motion together, her head now aligned with the rest of her body, eyes soft and responding to my energy and intention. She forgot about her horses and I forgot about my need to help her forget. We were merged souls, with whole brained integration and coherence like a mare and foal, moving together in the same direction as the seagulls soared and called out overhead and the breeze and now relaxed movement ruffled her blonde mane in its own stunning dance.

Helping Chasta to overcome her resistance has been one of the greatest challenges of my lifetime precisely because of my tremendous need to overcome *my own* unhealthy resistance patterns. Now I love to believe that we are helping each other as we both become more naturally accepting of life and the ability to go with the flow and flow with the go. And beyond the challenge comes the rewarding joy of one of the most intimately wondrous relationships that I have ever had—more than anything I could ever have imagined possible. And we are still just beginners on our journey and it is that mindset on our way to the lifetime practice of mastery that keeps us connected at a heart level. Chasta will not ever be likely to allow me to rest on my laurels (interestingly an expression that harkens back to the Olympic equestrian games of the ancient Greeks whose horses were adorned with wreaths of laurel), but directing me ever onward, as lead horses do with their own herd. So it is my privilege and responsibility to meet her there, our movement together becoming the dance of life.

Are her patterns of the need for resistance dissolving? Thankfully, a resounding *"Yes!" Thank God.* (and everyone else who has helped us on our path to partnership) And mine? Another *"Yes!"* Are there residues remaining? "Yes, again, *darn it!"* And they are sometimes dangerous. But life itself is dangerous and learning to interact with horses in a confident way is a calculated risk. Like snow skiing. Or even the mundane task of driving a car to work. If we really ever thought too much too long about the inherent risks in life, we might never come out from under the covers in the morning.

Do I have a death wish? *"Absolutely not."* I have a life wish! To live mine to the fullest, and as Pat Parelli says to his students, *"To be the very best Me that I can be!"* And in doing so, help Chasta to maintain her unique dignity by allowing her to be the spirit that was breathed into her by our mutual Creator.

God brought us together and I intend to let nature take its course.

Cold water, warm hearts

Photo by Kathy Yaeger

Connie and Chasta on Whidbey Island

Chapter Twelve

The Ten Percent Factor:
Still Horse Crazy
after all these Years

Chasta is a remarkable horse. No question about it. And though I believe deep in my heart that every living creature is a miracle, my horse is *unique.* She has shown me time and time again that her inner wheels are constantly turning with finely tuned sensibilities that are alert and aligned to all that is.

It seems like she works at appearing blasé and likes to maintain her stoic nature most of the time. Occasionally she looks at me like my attempts at playful games are entirely beneath her dignity with an expression of what appears to be "You have *got* to be kidding me!" If I am cleaning out the trailer after an outing and replacing the shavings and the horses are grazing nearby, I have been known to call out: *"First horse to come see me in the trailer gets a carrot!"* Immediately responding in a thumping into the trailer greeting is Gaela who will do practically anything for the crunchy orange vegetable. "Good *girl*, Gaela!" I smiled and stroked her ears while she chewed quickly, hoping for more. And then there was Chasta, standing at the back *outside* of the trailer, head poked in, reaching out toward me for her reward. "The game was coming *in* the trailer," I said aloud to Chasta as I ushered Gaela out, walking backwards as they have been taught to exit safely. Chasta responded with an "Oh, *brother*!" expression and walked away. Shortly after, I was in a nearby pasture scooping horse poop into my *Newer Spreader*™, a clever contraption that can be attached to any small farm vehicle and allows me to distribute manure in a very small pieces over the acreage, improving our soil and what sustains our horses. Fun, easy and environmentally friendly—right up my alley! Noticing a big green ball nearby that I had learned to incorporate into my horseplay by studying the Parelli Natural Horse. Man.Ship™ program, I hollered, *"First horse to touch the green ball with any body part gets a carrot!"* As I gave the horses a mental picture of them approaching and touching the ball, Gaela headed in my direction behind the ball and put her nose on it. "What a *clever* girl you are!" I said enthusiastically as I reach forward with her treat. Crunching away and pushing the ball to move it out of the way in an attempt for more, I stroked Gaela on her neck and asked Chasta if *she* wanted to play. She stuck her nose toward me without moving her feet, requesting a carrot. Again, I reminded her, the game was: *"Touch the ball, get a carrot."* But she walked away, looking totally uninterested while Gaela is thinking about what my next request might be. Should she walk over the logs I have lying like a huge spiked wheel on the ground? Those are always good for a carrot or chunk of juicy apple. Especially when she *backs* over them. Not Chasta. While Gaela walked over the logs at liberty to greet me on the other side with treats, Chasta deliberately walked *all the way* around them (which is considerably more work in its own right) while Gaela is enjoying her reward and sticks her nose in toward me, waiting for hers. By now you might be thinking that Gaela is a very intelligent and willing little horse. And *she is!* But it is *not* that Chasta is unable to do the things that I have just described. She can. *Easily!* It is just that she has to *want* to engage with me, to feel *motivated,* to know *why.* Sometimes when I block the trailer and leave the doors tied safely open, I hide (which is no easy task since Chasta *always* seems to be aware of where I am) and watch her trot inside to find the carrots planted in various places like an Easter Egg hunt, the same way that I notice her play with the big green ball or even walk over the logs on her own. But if she 'catches' me observing her, she will look away, yawn and appear hideously bored by it all. Not that I think that she is dishonest. *Not a bit!* As many of my favorite writers have expressed, horses don't lie. *She just is who she is.*

In this vein, Chasta *loves* to play and is extremely curious, yet likes to do it on the sly. While I am around, she leaves obstacles in their places and engages only with them at my suggestion. But leave her alone and out of my eyesight and she will turn the place entirely upside down. I have considered installing surveillance cameras since I am sure her pillaging would make an excellent video for YouTube.

The evening of the day Gaela eagerly played my games and Chasta wanted to play by her own rules, I went to help my parents with their dinner at a time in their lives when they needed ongoing assistance. They are both really great sports about hearing my unceasing animal tales and my father summed it up beautifully: "Why should Queen Chasta come off her royal throne to play the games that the court jester, Gaela, so eagerly does when they are beneath her dignity?! She needs new challenges—something worthy of her regal nature!" *Bravo!* Dad hit the nail on the head.

That is why Chasta is such a good teacher for me. I could *make* her do it---snap on a lead line and put pressure on her in a number of ways, both fair and just or forceful and cruel, (not an option for me) but at liberty, she made a choice to say *"No."* Some trainers would argue that your horse should *always* be obedient, and while I understand the logic of the fact that it is very important in a healthy partnership to have consistency since sometimes you and your horse could be in a life or death situation and you want the pattern of your leadership to be the deciding factor. Yet I have read many stories when a horse refused to obey their human and when pushed on, held their ground and it was because the human failed to know that they were approaching quicksand or some other life threatening circumstance *but the horse did*. We must be so aware of the fact that horses possess extreme intelligence and that we often fail to recognize it for what it is. Believe me when I tell you that Chasta makes *very* deliberate choices! I am learning *so* much from Linda Parelli who is a *fabulous* natural horsewoman and has an ability to observe the nature of each individual horse and instead of feeling frustrated, afraid or mad, can pause long enough to say, *"How interesting!"* before making a decision how best to respond to the situation. With Chasta, I have often said, "How *fascinating!"*

Yet I was *offering* this game to my horses, not demanding that anyone play. The reward was a treat and extra affection in the form of scratches. But there was no punishment or withdrawal of affection. Gaela chose "play and get a treat" and Chasta wanted her own version of "no play and get a treat." *"Doesn't work that way, Pal,"* I reminded her. But daily I give my horses a few unearned treats (not to mention their healthy pasture, natural supplements and fresh abundant water from the greatest non-electric horse drinker in the world, (Bar-Bar-A™) and scratches and grooming to remind them that they are *always* loved---*not for what they do but for who they are*. Yet Chasta continues to challenge me to think outside the box. As Pat Parelli says, "We need to be provocative enough for our horses so that they *want* to be with us." With Chasta, that remains my ongoing challenge and delight.

When my son Evan was teaching me how to hook up my horse trailer, it felt very intimidating to me. What comes completely naturally to a young man who understands and relates to machines and metal parts made me feel completely brainless. As he patiently explained the steps *again* to his fumbling mother, his car racing coach (herself an accomplished multiple time champion driver who beat scores of men more than twice her size) who was visiting walked up behind us and quietly said, *"Ten percent factor"* out of the corner of her mouth as a grin covered my son's handsome face. "What's that?" I questioned, aware they had yet another private joke between them, their world of race cars and mechanics totally foreign to me. "You have to be ten percent smarter than what you are working with to be able to succeed," she said, the corners of her mouth turning up and a twinkle in her eye. "Hmmmm..." I thought, surely with time and practice, I could overcome this perceived difficulty and have it become a simple task. It made me smile.

Until I thought of Chasta. Smarter than my horse? *Hardly!!* Although I have a college degree, she outsmarts me constantly. She notices *everything*. Once Chasta and I attended a workshop in Canada with master horseman Jonathan Field (Jonathan Field Horsemanship™). In the early morning before the clinic started, my friend Dolores Elliason had done an equine bodywork session with

Chasta which left her very relaxed and soft, nearly dozing. When it was finished, I looked at my watch and realized the workshop was about to start in fifteen minutes and I needed to use the restroom. After thanks and compensation, I securely tied a sleepy Chasta to my trailer, and headed to the far end of the stable. When I returned, Dolores approached me and asked why I had allowed Chasta to graze at liberty behind the parking lot—with total access to the open road and the wild blue yonder. Thinking she may have mixed up Chasta with another similar looking horse, I told her that Chasta was tied quietly to my trailer. Dolores, very clever in ways that remind me of Chasta, said, *"Take a look!"* as she pointed a finger. There was Chasta, far off in the distance grazing in a field of tall grass behind the parking lot. The only way to have accessed it from where she had been was to untie herself from the trailer and walk, dragging her lead rope, directly through the maze of arriving trailers, people walking horses, dogs and barn cats, staff and wheelbarrows of manure and even Jonathan, leaned up against his own trailer visiting with his students. *How could no one have noticed?!* Does she have an invisibility cloak like Harry Potter?!

I approached her slowly walking at an arc,

catching her eye, which was watching me closely as her head remained on the ground, inhaling the tender spring grass. She picked her right front hoof up and actually tapped it on the ground next to a beautiful feather, which I picked up in awe and wonder. "*You* are a *very* smart horse," I stammered, feeling that familiar sensation like I had been given an amazing yet *truly* complicated gift. "*I know,*" I swear she said in reply as we walked into the arena to start the day.

Since my mother was diagnosed with Parkinson's disease, she had lost much of her strength and balance in a very short period, which was incredibly distressing to all of us. She had wonderful memories about riding gentle horses with her sister as a child on a family farm in Canada and described it to me in vivid detail with happy recall. She had not been on a horse's back since those halcyon summer days. I asked her if she wanted to have a ride in the round corral where she would be safe and we could work on trying to strengthen her balance. She surprised me by not only saying an emphatic "*Yes!*" but by choosing Chasta over Ritzy, the older and more well seasoned horse without an explosive history. With my father as spotter, we got her up into my most secure saddle, thankful she was so petite and began to walk slowly along the rails. "When and if you feel ready," I said softly, " lean forward a bit and place your hands over her withers and if you feel *really* brave, close your eyes and allow the wonderful movement to flow up into your body and just relax into it." Mom set her jaw with a determined look and I noticed that soon after she closed her eyes tentatively and within a half lap around the ring she slowly started to soften and the tension in her face began to relax. Soon without opening her eyes, she asked quietly if we could slow down a little since she was feeling a bit dizzy. Before I had a chance to respond, Chasta immediately squared herself up under my mother and slowed her tempo, looking over at me as if to say she had it all under control. I asked Mom if she wanted to stop, and she smiled weakly, eyes still closed, and whispered *"No."* With a huge lump in my throat, we proceeded for awhile until the expression on her face looked entirely childlike and dreamy through closed lids. Again, before I had the chance to make the decision to end the session, Chasta came to a careful stop, knowing that her timing was perfect and then stood quietly for a long time while my mother opened her eyes wide as if rediscovering some very special part of herself. Then as we struggled to get her down out of the saddle up from the top of sixteen hands of sqookum horseflesh, Chasta stood squared and erect like a soldier and when Mom's feet touched the ground, softened and wrapped her neck around her and held her in the space a mare does her foal. It was one of the most beautiful gestures I have ever witnessed and my mother stood, at a time when she was usually very unsteady on her feet, and wept in gratitude and buried her head in this remarkable animal for the longest time while I stood back in awe. Chasta had and *knew* her purpose and was rock solid in her strength.

And when Gaela was new to us, she bonded *intensely* with Chasta, and did not want to be out of her sight. Because of this, I asked Chasta if she would please stand quietly tied into her stall while my friend Kathy did Gaela's first natural barefoot hoof trim. The doors to their stalls are always open so they have the choice to come and go freely. Tying Chasta to the iron bars, I thanked her and took hold of Gaela's lead line so Kathy could get to work. Because her beloved herd mate was clearly visible a few feet away behind the half door, Gaela relaxed and allowed the procedure, her nerves calmed by Chasta's presence. After we finished, I went to get Chasta, and told her that I really appreciated how quietly she had stood and waited for nearly an hour and then opened the door and reached up to untie her rope. Stunned, I looked down to see it hanging limply on the rubber mat of her stall! She had not moved an inch and I had been so absorbed in helping Gaela to relax that I had missed Chasta's actions. *Believe me*, no horse should have been able to untie this knot without extraordinary attention! Standing there with my mouth open, she looked at me as if to say, *"You did not have to tie me, just ask and trust me."*

This is a horse who has the capacity to open gates daily if she choses to and has even stayed within her fencelines on a few occasions when there was "operator error" on my part by failing to close or securely latch a gate behind me. She stands tied quietly whenever and wherever I ask on a regular basis with no resistance or shenanigans whatsoever. She routinely ground ties in place with the lead rope resting limply without being secured, when I walk away and expect her to stay in place. She is also willing to do that at liberty, when the spirit moves her and my leadership is enough.

Several stunning examples of her deliberate choices occurred back to back in the same week recently. With my parents' ongoing health difficulties, my fatigue and ongoing concern was considerable and I longed for the peace and joy of being in nature with my horse. Not able to find any of my friends to buddy with, I told Chasta that it was just the two of us and that my heart wanted to be with her on a trail ride to the mountains, which I believe is her favorite outing and she rewarded me with impeccable connection and exhuberance, every bit the steady horse of my dreams, wearing only a rope halter and responding beautifully to all transitions. As Pat Parelli would say, Chasta's "whoa" equalled her "go" which made her a joy to ride, my mare's Tennessee Walker blood swinging us up and down fluidly with an extra skip in her step that the nicer weather was finally upon us on this glorious sunny afternoon. Following the mountain ride, we swam in the lake below together, the golden horse swimming alongside two yellow labs chasing floating rubber bones with their human. As my friend Judy says, "It was a slice of Heaven." *For both of us.* And I believe that Chasta fully knew what it meant to me. Stepping out of the water, she was a deep butterscotch color dripping wet and most everyone on the beach came to admire her while she calmly accepted and enjoyed their curiosity and approval. Chasta offered extra attention and quiet patience to a small wide eyed boy with special needs whose mother said he had never seen a horse up close before.

Then the next day I took my parents out for a special outing to celebrate Mother and Father's Days on my Dad's actual birthday and planned to finish with a 'horse show' at the end of our time together. When we were getting close to our place, I started to think about how difficult it is to get them both in and out of the car since Parkinson's disease and my father's stroke has affected their motor functions considerably. And getting them comfortably seated also posed a challenge so I had a sudden inspiration—I would drive my car directly into the pasture where the obstacle course awaited us. Sort of like Wild Safari Park but with horses, dogs, cats and ducks! Parking at an angle and rolling down the windows, I gave Chasta and Gaela a mental picture that my parents were in the car and that I hoped they would really put on a great show, knowing how much their audience would love it. Then I ran into the house to get some carrots for my parents to reward them with—sort of the price of admission.

When I came out, Chasta was whinnying at me impatiently like *"Let's get this show on the road!!"* so I hurried over to the pasture where they were standing at the gate and led them to the car and their 'showground'---they poked their noses into the open windows to say hello and while Gaela gobbled her carrot down and nosed around for more, Chasta ate hers gingerly but looked at them with doe brown eyes, suggesting that it was not a necessary offering — that she was *their gift*. As I walked toward the obstacle course, she collected herself vertically and pranced like a dressage horse, not something that I have been able to ask her to offer me. For all the world, she looked like she was saying, "Am I not *magnificent?!*" And she *was*, light as a feather and attentive to her audience from inside the car, clapping and saying *"Good girl!"* in appreciative voices. In that moment, I knew that my parents were talking to Chasta, yet I felt like a small child, being noticed and appreciated and my heart soared.

Then I took off the lead line for our finale at liberty — she went over jumps and walked forward and backward through the labyrinth and then sidepassed three barrels with complete ease while I sat on another barrel twenty feet away — I tried to set her equine form up to succeed with my own body language gestures but she did it mostly on her own, leaving me to marvel in awe and wonder with tears in my eyes that this horse was aiming to *give herself to them for their pleasure* for a birthday gift and an awareness of their debilitation and dignity. She had never gone sideways over three barrels in both directions at liberty before that day!

When it was Gaela's turn, Chasta stood a few feet from the car window at liberty and watched us intently, head still vertically collected as if she was very proud and seeming to offer silent support to her young charge. She did not graze in the lush June grass under her feet, but gave Geala a chance to shine, their usual competition set aside. When we finished and showed them Gaela's gains in her confidence with her games, we walked over at liberty and picked Chasta up to connect with us and went to the windows so my mother and father could give them a pet and another carrot. Chasta only seemed to take the carrot demurely to be polite, and nodded to them gratefully. Then she turned and put her nose gently on Gaela and drove her away toward the lower pasture where they resumed their afternoon as grazing beauties. Again, this sense of a purpose for Chasta to *please them* seemed to be all in day's work.

The following afternoon I had a visit from a dear young girl named Grace who fell in love with Chasta on a school field trip here and had begged her mother since to return. I volunteered to spend time with her, sharing my love for what I am learning about these amazing creatures. Chasta surveyed her newest little friend and noticed *immediately* that this little human *adored* her. Chasta stood patiently while I yammered on, explaining the Parelli philosophy of always applying pressure in phases, starting with the lightest possible to get a response. With focused intention, I wiggled my finger lightly to ask Chasta to back up, which she normally easily responds to, but she looked at me lazily like it was all so incredibly boring that she might just fall asleep on the spot, and wake up mercifully when it was all over. So I had to increase the pressure by wiggling my wrist and then got only a reluctant few steps backwards so needed to get my elbow swinging to get any real results. When she stood at the end of the line, I waited for her to show some connection, and then asked her to return to me, which she did without any particular enthusiasm and an exaggerated yawn.

Then it was Grace's turn. I reminded her to focus and start with just the tiniest wiggle, but to be prepared to ask for a response by increasing it if necessary. Grace took a deep breath and looking at Chasta with total awe, wiggled her tiny finger back and forth. Chasta shot straight back like she suddenly wanted to play the game with her whole heart while Grace smiled with wide eyed wonder that she had just moved a 1200 pound animal as if she were a feather! When she asked her to return, this gorgeous golden mare fairly trotted to reunite with her new friend who enthused, "That was *fun!!*" while her mother stood exclaiming—"*Omigosh*—what a *smart* horse to give Grace the perfect response so she could sense what it was *supposed* to feel like!" She was also quite amused that she did *not* offer it to me! It was not as if I had primed the pump---Chasta made a *decision.* Smart horse, indeed! It made me ask the question---what would *I* have to do to be more like Grace? Likely come from my heart more and yammer less, for starters…

A number of years ago, the only time I have ever (I know that I am tempting fate by mentioning this, especially in print) come off Chasta, as in "parting company" (You get the picture) was sort of a combination of simultaneously being thrown and attempting to bail. It was completely lacking in grace or fluidity, though I had previously practiced my emergency dismounts. I had been riding her bareback in a large pasture, working diligently to develop my independent seat and creating patterns in my mind to ride at the trot and canter. At some point she apparently lost patience with my ineptitude and took off, galloping wildly toward a fence. I had survived a number of previous runaways in our early days that could have had devastating consequences and this outburst seemed to have that dreadful potential so I grabbed some mane and attempted to swing off and land on my feet but awkwardly hit the ground hard on one hip instead, followed by my head, feeling grateful I was wearing a hard hat. She stopped and looked at me as I laid there and for some reason I felt weirdly relieved and calm. By rights, I should have fallen from horses many times, since my riding experience is limited, but most of them had attempted to help me. Chasta, in that moment, clearly had not. Maybe if I had quit our session sooner, been more attentive to her signals earlier, given her more time to rest between requests, noticed her efforts better, been lighter with my seat and hands, remained in a smaller space until we had a stronger connection, improved our transitions on the ground at liberty….. What is it they say about hindsight, especially when you are on yours looking up from the dirt?!

I knew that I wasn't dead (!) not even badly hurt, and felt immensely grateful for that but disappointed by her behavior after how hard I had consistently tried to be a better partner and work on my leadership. Surprisingly tranquil, I did not act mean or mad, but decided she needed a "time out", like a child who needs to think about their tantrum as much as I needed to think about what I had to do to improve my skills. *Trust me,* I am well aware *at all times* that Chasta is a horse and I am a human and that there are considerable differences in our behavior patterns as species. But I also believe that that we are connected deeply by our common emotions and that we both have an enormous instinct to survive but also *to help each other do so through our loving bond.*

"This is what assertive feels like" I noted to myself as I led her to the round corral, tying her to a post. I wished that I had better known that assertive feeling horseback as well, but this is the way that I continue to improve. Puffing out my chest, my emphatic message seemed clear: "I would like you to think about your behavior and our partnership and how much I am continuing to try to do my very best for both of us" I stated matter-of factly. To many, this sounds like *complete* anthropomorphism at its worst (or best?!) but *on some level*, I believe that she knew *exactly what I meant and how I felt.* Then I closed the wooden latch and the gate and clamped on a small rope with a metal clasp

around it. Just for good measure. So that she knew I was setting a boundary. That I *meant* it. *No punishment*, simply quiet time for both of us.

Gathering my wits, I began to also pick up the groom box and its contents to be put away. Puttering around for a short time, trying to calmly process what had just happened, taking the pressure off my sore hip by walking on the other leg, I hung up my hardhat and tidied up the tack room a bit. It could not have been more than a half an hour later when I emerged and looked over my shoulder to see if Chasta's posture was at all contrite before I released her.

For a moment, I thought I must have hit my head harder than I realized. It felt like I was seeing an optical illusion. She was grazing contentedly about ten feet *outside* the open gate to the round corral. She had, in this order: untied herself from the fencepost which defies any odds, chewed through the small rope around the doweled gate latch, which had hit the ground and was covered with horse slobber, then opened the gate by sliding the dowel across with her teeth and let herself out, dragging her lead rope on the ground. Did she escape? No. She was eating happily and *watching me watch her*, nose to the ground *just outside* the boundary that I had set for her. Was she telling me that I could tie her body but not her spirit? She could have left the area. Instead, she left me standing there, mouth gaping, feeling as if I was crazy.

And I guess that's it. *I am*. Still horse crazy after all these years.

Wild Blue Yonder

Photo by Kathy Yaeger

Chapter Thirteen

Lighten Up

Ritzy, our Egyptian Arabian horse was an extremely gentle and loving animal with an incredibly generous spirit. He *always* nickered to me when I approached in a hearty hello and softly in goodbye whenever I left and *every single time* I was thrilled---I never tired of his friendliness and tried to be aware not to take it for granted. He was always heading for me as I walked in his direction— often at the trot! My presence represented good things in his mind and I never met a horse who loved to be touched more than he did which made grooming him a joyful experience that always made my day. He showed me with his half closed eyes, droopy lips and rapturous expressions that he loved our time together and I did my best to let him know how heavenly and therapeutic it was for me, too. *Sigh.*

Arabian horses have been bred throughout the centuries to live in close proximity to their human families in intimate ways and it has shaped their collective demeanor as a breed that is particularly loving and loyal and Ritzy was a classic example of this devotion. He always forgave my awkward attempts to learn to handle ropes, my muddy signals that he tried his best to decipher and to develop my often unbalanced riding seat---he aimed to please. He helped me *immeasurably* to improve my skills and confidence.

In his senior years, Ritzy developed a metabolic condition known as Cushing's disease that includes a problematic symptom of creating the inability to shed out their winter hair that becomes unnaturally thick and curly. He was unable to return to the sleek and smooth liver chestnut coat that he had always sported in the summers and I was forced to buy a pair of heavy duty shearers as regular horse trimmers just would not cut through the dense hair.

I expect my animals to respect the time and space that I give to each one of them while grooming or having their hooves trimmed by standing quietly and allowing the animal who is on the receiving end privacy and my full attention. No mooching for carrots or pushing in for a rub with their noses.

This new shearer was a big contraption with

a heavy duty cord and I took Ritzy behind the stable and proceeded to get started. The first swath across his side startled me — it peeled off in a huge clump like pulling apart a flake of hay---I felt as if I was shearing a woolly sheep! Ritzy stood calmly and patiently as I struggled to adjust to this heavy and unwieldy motorized machine that was moving across his barrel removing the curly locks like a lawnmower. I attempted to be light and careful with my strokes, but it was difficult to maneuver and it did not take either of us long to work up a sweat, especially during the heat of the day.

After a time, I had made good progress when Chasta approached and put her head under my arms at the elbow and nudged upwards. "Hello, girl — please allow Ritzy his time---this is his turn---this thing is dangerous so give us some space." She repeated her nudge so I quietly pushed her off with hand gestures and a stern *"not now"* look. She walked away only to return a few minutes later to repeat the process closer to my wrists this time and I cut the power, stroked Ritzy for his patience and said, "Chasta, you will be brushed in a few more minutes---this is *Ritzy's* time." She did not budge so I shooed her away with a bit more vigor and resumed my project, earnestly attempting to give Ritzy comfort by removing this thick blanket of hair as the daily temperatures continued to climb.

Working away intently, I hardly noticed Chasta's approach for the third time but when I looked up we were eye to eye. Her gaze was firm as if she meant business and before I had time to respond, she clamped her teeth over my hands that held the shearer. "*Enough*. That is enough for today" came the message, now abundantly clear.

This wasn't about her and a need for attention. It was not about me and my desire to get the job done, however good my intentions. It was about Ritzy, standing quietly with the patience of Job on a blistering hot day. My heart was in the right place, but my human direct line thinking to 'get the job done' was in the way of my need to pay attention to what I was asking of my horse. So often I approach life as if I am "on a mission"---not noticing subtle cues that advise me to slow down to smell the roses along the way or in this case, to shear Ritzy over several shorter sessions and not just because I had a fancy new shearer that could do the job in one fell swoop.

Chasta noticed that he was laboring to tolerate this heavy, noisy machine. A younger horse in better health could have more easily accepted it, but for him, it was difficult. I had praised him along the way for standing quietly but had failed to read his cues that he would *love* a break.

Chasta held my hand in her teeth, not with any force, but with complete purpose. Trust me, anyone who knows horses realizes if they decide to bite, they can crush flesh and bone. I turned off the switch and stood transfixed. "You are right, Chasta. He needs a rest. *Thank you for helping me to see that.*"

The moment that I finally became aware of the communication, she released her teeth and took a step back and turned to Ritzy, her best friend and life mate. He had been allowing me to do this for him with a halter and his lead rope hanging on the ground untied. He could have walked away or at least gotten antsy the entire time but he did neither and I had praised him for his patience. But did I want, however sincerely, to cross something off my "to do" list as much as I wanted to be aware of his thresholds of comfort and tolerance?

Ritzy looked at Chasta as if to say *"Thanks, Pal!"* while she gently rubbed his muzzle with her nose and then they both looked at me.

Humbled and choked up to tears at their mutual tenderness, I placed the shearers on a nearby tree stump. "Enjoy your afternoon in the sunshine, you two. Thanks for looking out for each other and for teaching me *so* many things. I love you both." They each took a few steps in my direction in unison and offered me their heads for my strokes of affection. Then they turned, as one, and walked away.

Looking at all of the hair on the ground at my feet, I realized we were all much lighter for the experience.

Chasta and Ritzy: *Best Friends*

Chapter Fourteen

My Funny Valentine

Gaela came into my life because I dreamed her up in my heart and mind when I was seven and God blessed me with her physical presence in reality when I was fifty-two.

Loving horses of every size, shape and color as a child, I was especially attracted to Palominos, Buckskins and spotted horses of all descriptions. The imaginary ponies that I drew and dreamed of constantly often had spots in the shapes of hearts, and why not? God gave us all a creative spirit to express our hearts, and mine are often literal.

The first day that I met Gaela it was love at first sight. Not a rational, carefully considered thinking process, rather a mutual recognition that we were meant to be together. She was a rescue horse with an uncertain pedigree and I was so busy falling in love that she seemed to morph into my past-present-future simultaneously as my heart began to beat faster. I was startled by the ferocity of my feelings and how much I wanted to love and protect this young little horse and receive her affection.

I felt her soft gaze on me confirming our connection as she slowly turned and seemed to deliberately show me her heart. Not the one pumping blood through her system, but the large chocolate colored spot on her left hindquarters in a perfectly shaped furry heart. She was my dream come true standing right in front of me.

My educated guess is that Gaela is a Mustang-Arab cross due to her compact and sturdy build and Roman nose and unmistakable eye characterized by the Mustang and her incredibly fluid movement that feels absolutely Arab. She is a complete contortionist with rapid-fire moves that can occur in a millisecond. She loves to roll and itch her back and adjust her own spine and gives it such determined effort that when she is finished with her furious back and forth movement, she rocks onto her feet and does a huge leap like a wild stag or a well-trained Lippizanner stallion performing airs above the ground. That is followed by a few mighty bucks to get the kinks out of her hindquarters and bowels since there are usually a series of accompanying staccato farts. All this she does while glancing furtively in all directions lest there be something invading her ritual territory. I have dubbed this her "Groucho Marx look" since her dark eyes are topped with black outlines like wide eyebrows. One moment she is stunningly beautiful to me and the next I expect to see her in wire glasses with round rims and a fat cigar like the famous vaudevillian comedian. Gaela is the ultimate extrovert, like Groucho, and I am blessed with her entertainment. She even has a remarkably deep voice when she nickers which is completely out of proportion to her size and sounds *hilarious,* adding to the comparison. In fact, I can easily hear her say one of Groucho's most famous one-liners: *"You can quote me on saying that I was misquoted."* I am sure that horses feel that way a lot as we humans try our best to interpret them and just plain miss the mark.

And as with Chasta, we had her previous trauma to overcome and heal. She acted far more high strung than I believed was her true calm and steady nature. With time and patience to develop our bond, her willing and friendly ways have come to the forefront of our relationship. I especially thank Carolyn Resnick, author of *Naked Liberty*, for emphasizing spending time sharing space at liberty in an undemanding way with my horses to contributing to this amazing bond. Carolyn has a wonderful ongoing blog on her website, where she shares her fantastic philosophy and depth of knowledge and experience. It inspires and informs me regularly, continually challenging me to be the wise and balanced leader that my horses need and deserve me to be. After what I am learning from the Parellis and Carolyn and others, I realized that this communication is the basis for everything that follows and it was the mistake I made so dreadfully with Chasta in the early days of our time together when I attempted to saddle and ride her long before I had earned the privilege of her consent to do so. With Gaela, much of our time was spent at liberty in the beginning (and still is!) and she was given a choice to interact or not, and as a result, she offered me so much more very quickly. I spent a lot of time taking Chasta aside and reminding her that if I had known better, I would have offered her the same and that now I can and do. I whispered this into her ears while scratching her under her jowl, which this formally headshy mare now loves. Fortunately for me, God made horses exceptionally forgiving, and are teaching me to be the same---with myself and others.

Because Gaela had more aware handling due to the strides forward I am making in my savvy, she has become a little mountain goat on the trails and all of our practice at home with countless obstacles on our "Horse Course" playground has helped her to become remarkably unflappable. I have loved to watch her progress to *not* respond by spooking and running wildly to sudden noises and movement. We keep a large metal garbage can inside the fenced gates of our gardens that holds grain for the ducks that live in and around our pond. The lid can make a loud clanging noise and one day after filling the can, a huge gust of wind got under the heavy paper sack and lifted it away from me and caused it to flutter across the fence noisily. Gaela spooked and spun, wild eyed, like she had seen a ghost and ran at top speed and hid behind Chasta for protection. Her lead mare, Chasta, had never even lifted her head from the grass while grazing over the commotion that had Gaela so worried.

Chasta's calm response was *not* always the case. She is the same horse, who when new to us, almost ran into the next county when I approached her with a *carrot* and broke it in half from twenty feet away! The attack of the killer carrot had to become a dance of approach and retreat and I needed to walk *away* from her, breaking the carrot into pieces until she accepted them as edible instead of a threat! Her confidence level at present makes it difficult to even *get* a reaction, which makes her a great leader for young Gaela.

So due to Gaela's anxiety over the noisy, abrupt change in her environment, I spent the next ten minutes walking the fencelines with the grain sack, deliberately banging it up and down and across, making a similar commotion to what had originally frightened her, while making no eye contact and minding my own business, which is what I had been doing in the first place when feeding the ducks. Continuing until she was no longer bothered and commending Chasta for her total relaxation, I rewarded Gaela by stopping and giving her praise in the form of petting for her calmness.

Finally, walking toward her with the sack, I rubbed it all over her back and down her legs and under her belly. Fortunately there was a handful of grain in the bottom of the sack to give her a special reward for her efforts to remain calm. As I walked away, I left the sack in a place that I felt she would explore it on her own and banged the can lid a few more times for good measure. Just as I had predicted, as I looked back, she had her nose inside the grain sack, looking for more, and suddenly, Chasta shared her interest!

Within a fairly short period, the noisy metal can, unexpected or not, was no big deal for her and the first day when she actually "spooked in place" when surprised by it was a huge victory for us. Her body reacted in a startled jolt of adrenaline from the sudden noise but her legs were *planted*. She was *physically* wired to be a cautious prey animal, ready to flee possible danger, but she was *emotionally* collected, responding to now familiar changes in her environment. I was so delighted that from behind the fence, I called to her after tossing a bowlful of grain to the ducks. "Come here, Gaela! That was *so brave!* I have a treat for you!"

She walked to me, head forward, on a mission to get her reward and when I looked down over the fence that had blocked my view as she drew closer, I noticed that her knees were absolutely *knocking!* Her entire lower body was shaking as she absorbed the shot of adrenaline from her reactionary right brain, but she had learned to park herself long enough to access in her rational left brain the ability to determine whether she was in any *real* danger. Those are the breakthrough moments that remain so tender in building relationships! I gave her an extra handful of grain, which she gobbled happily, her pretty spotted chest puffed out in pride, while her heart beat like a hummingbird!

Gaela represents the eternal child to me. Not because she is a young horse, rather that she possesses an open and curious, friendly spirit. Each day she inspires me to feel young and reborn. She has been so good for me in terms of having an open, hopeful, and curious lens about the process of life, especially in these uncertain times in which we live. But can we reframe that to realize that this is a very exciting time in history to be alive? How can we remain open and curious to the process of life and let go of our need for the certainty of the outcome? To learn to live in peace in the midst of chaos. To remain anchored in hope and faith and the inherent goodness and resiliency of the human spirit rather than on its potential for darkness. Ask yourself who or what in your life can help you perceive life through an open, curious and hopeful lens. Is it an animal, a child, conscious contact with God through meditation and prayer, exercise, inspirational reading? Commit to spending time with it daily while I take a break and go find Gaela — or simply think about her and smile and find my perspective again…

Gaela rewarded the hours and hours of patience that it takes to help expose a horse to stimulation that can provoke fear and panic by carefully presenting things in a way that builds the left side of the brain to think through a potential problem rather than go immediately into fight and flight when we had a winter storm and she got her leg trapped in a strong cord rope. The challenge was, the cord was attached to a fence. When I first met Gaela, she was very worried about ropes or anything that moved in general, especially near her hindquarters, and when I introduced them, she wanted to run away or immediately disengage her hindquarters to remove the offending pressure. Because of her fears, I slowly and methodically introduced her to countless sensations with ropes up and down and around her legs, watchful of her thresholds and praising her by removing the stimulus whenever she showed relaxation and understanding. I stroked her with feathers, jingled bells back there, asked her to walk through deep piles of leaves and sand, rubbed pool noodles on her legs as well as fallen evergreen branches and anything else that I could think of. Water from the hose, organic bug spray, and all manner of things, but especially ropes. I led her feet wrapped in rope to move forward and back and side to side. She made wonderful strides and most all of the time she seemed remarkably confident. And yet you never know for sure with horses until you are tested.

The week of a heavy snow gave us that opportunity. In order to help the horses maintain their body heat in the freezing weather, I was feeding them four times a day and when I went out for the late afternoon ration, Chasta called to me at the fence in a tone that meant that she was more than hungry. When I asked her where Gaela was, she took me there at liberty as I held out two buckets of oats, their favorite treat. Chasta looked at her bucket wistfully, but knew Gaela needed me, so carried on. There she was, way back against a temporary fence that we had done when we changed the shape of our composting area and had not managed to get the round rail wooden fence in the ground before winter. She was standing under a huge tree, looking very tiny under her seldom needed blanket in snow a foot deep. She saw her bucket, but made no attempt to come forward to it. *Strange.* Yet I already knew from Chasta's behavior that something was wrong. "Hey, Gaela. I'm coming. *What is it*, girl?" As Chasta and I approached, she carefully put her right hind foot up and I could see that it was completely wrapped tight around her fetlock in the white cord that was as thick as my pinky finger. There was no sign of a struggle, and she simply stood patiently waiting for me to help her. *Incredible!* When I got to her side, she stood quietly on three legs while I unwrapped the cord, and I praised her and put the oats down, telling her aloud how very proud I was that she made a decision to stay calm and allow me to help her. She looked pleased and *very grown up* and dug into the oats while I surveyed her leg and the surrounding area. She was absolutely fine and I could easily see what had happened. A huge snow laden branch had snapped off one of the hundred year old Douglas Fir trees and landed on the cord, which caused it to pop out of its guide and onto the white snow. Anyone who knows the strength of horses realizes that if panic had been her response, she could have pulled the entire fence down. It was non-electric with temporary metal posts, but could have created a terrible wreck. Chasta's footprints were at the scene, too, so it made me wonder if she was responsible for helping to convince her charge that I would be out soon enough…..

With horses and with life, an ounce of prevention is worth a pound of cure and I am so grateful to what I am learning from the Parelli program about "prior and proper preparation." And the incredible value of the bond that Carolyn Resnick stresses above all else.

Recently, I enjoyed a session with Linda-Ann Bowling, an equine guided development specialist, to delve into those characteristics possessed by both human and horse based on Asian symbology. According to our most dominant natural traits, Gaela is the wind sign and I am the fire. Both are considered extroverted signs and could be a very potent combination yet my primary trait is determination and hers is flexibility which we can enhance in each other. My time with Linda-Ann was very provocative and fascinating and truly confirmed what a gift Gaela is in my life.

But it was not until I returned home that it occurred to me that there was a remarkable synchronicity to what Linda-Ann had guided me to discover about my partnership with Gaela. I recalled back to the time when she had been living with us only about a month that we had some extensive tree trimming done on our acreage after severe storms had broken huge tree limbs and felled some entire trees.

Since Gaela had made great early progress settling in and yet remained still remarkably spooky at the same time, I decided that rather than keeping the horses away from the commotion in another pasture, that I would spend the two days with them right in the middle of it. The men and trucks rumbled through the gates with their noisy motors and rattling chains, raised cherry picker buckets, florescent vests and hard hats while the herd of three, one human and two horses, took it all in. My message to my horses was clear: *"These men are here to help, and though we have to be watchful, we are completely safe and this can be an interesting process."* I modeled that in my mind and body. Allowing them to be at liberty since they had plenty of space for escape, the men were aware of them and eager to spend a few days in their midst. In fact, they were happy to have the horses become curious enough to come close in order to get a treat or scratch and survey their equipment, realizing how this was very useful to their development as safe saddle horses. At that time, Gaela was sure that Chasta, as her primary herdmate, represented her safety, so if Chasta took off, she was at her heels. Yet my leadership for Chasta became necessary when *her* thresholds for safety were pushed by all of the chaotic activity and she began to run to *me* for comfort. *What a payoff* this was for the three of us as they stood by me, unrestrained, calm and curious, and I could feel their bodies shudder with mine at the precise moment a gigantic limb came crashing to the ground from a safe distance.

Instead of running, they chose to watch with me in fascination. Because the huge limbs were too large to go into our chipper shredder, I hauled them until I had created three enormous piles and started fires in each one. As the winds picked up and began to howl, I became their icon of safety, (a description borrowed from the legendary Pat Parelli), and if I chose to stand warming myself by the fires, they did too, right by my side. By the end of day two, Gaela was walking a tight circle around the fires at liberty with me as they popped and crackled, watching the wind create dancing flames in apparent fascination, the dry cedar creating a scent to remember. In this recollection, I realized those two days where fire and wind were the theme, that we had formed an incredible and significant bond from exposure to those amazing and life giving elements that had literally set the stage for our partnership. *Fascinating!* I emailed Linda-Ann, who was delighted, *yet not surprised*, knowing intimately the magic of the interspecies bond as a path for discovery.

We had another breakthrough a few months later when I was finishing a play session on the obstacle course by asking her to walk backwards and squeeze through a narrow gate and pause there. She was willing to enter it walking backwards but resisted when I asked her to remain standing calmly in the middle for a few minutes. She squirted forward and back to relieve herself of the claustrophobic pressure while I calmly redirected her and gave her rest when she stood still in place and relaxed in between the narrow opening. No sooner had I released any pressure to confirm that she had made the choice that I had requested that she chewed and licked in understanding and acceptance when a large truck came up our driveway at a good clip, crunching the gravel noisily under the tires. This sudden movement in her blind spot was more than she thought she could handle in that vulnerable position and in a nanosecond began to move out of the gate toward me when I gently blocked her with a calm reminder that I could see the truck and to trust me enough to feel assured that it meant no danger to us. She looked *directly* at me, which allowed her to see my smiling face and confident posture. Her raised neck and enlarged eyes receded and she dropped her head and blew from within the narrow gate. I stood next to my young mare while she was squeezed in between, stroking her while I spoke to the gentleman in the truck for the next several minutes until we were so relaxed that we could have napped. The softness in her eye and body told me that her level of acceptance and understanding had really taken another leap forward. Yet her body was content to remain still in between the gate, a *huge* choice for her since a horse's instinct to fear is forward movement away from enclosed spaces.

Her trust in my leadership was confirmed the following morning when I went out to give them breakfast and found Chasta and Gaela sound asleep side by side on the ground in the pasture. Because lying down is a very vulnerable position to a prey animal, I was always aware of being relaxed in my intention as I approached. Happily, Gaela had allowed me to lay with her on several occasions previous to this, taking her cue from the fact that I frequently rested on the ground with Chasta. As I drew near, Chasta opened her eyes sleepily and rumbled a soft greeting which caused Gaela to flick an ear in my direction. Calmly, I bent down and scratched Gaela's neck and knelt on the ground next to her. She started to stretch and I felt a pang of disappointment, thinking that she was getting to her feet, so I quietly rolled over to give her enough space. Instead, for the first time in my close presence, she went from the lying pose that resembles an Egyptian Sphinx to completely flat down on her side. Oh, *joy!* This was what I had *so* waited for! Chasta watched us tenderly, recognizing my sheer delight and deep honor. Attempting to mirror her movement, I did the same thing until my body was lying on the grass directly next to her as she watched me with interest. In the next moment, I felt like human Jello when she rolled her head in my direction and gave a sigh of contentment, her eye inches from mine as both of our heads were on the ground, facing one another. In that moment, we realized that we were one with each other, the ground below us and the morning sky above, with our golden friend, Chasta, as sacred witness and likely the reason that this level of intimacy was possible between us.

That level of trust continued to build a few weeks later when we took a trail ride to one of my favorite places on a nearby mountain. Gaela was totally relaxed and curious the entire time, a steady partner and joy to ride. Coming back down the trails after working up quite a sweat, it seemed the perfect time for a swim in the lake below. It was obvious to me that she was unfamiliar with water other than the small and fairly shallow puddle crossings that I had worked with her on. Yet her new level of acceptance caused her to check with me and after receiving my reassurance, being willing to try.

Not caring that I hadn't brought a a change of clothes, I took my time and gave her plenty of line on the ground after removing her tack as we walked into the water together. Allowing her to explore it with her hooves and mouth, I started to float on my back and kick out at the end of the line. She seemed so surprised to see me in that position that the next thing I knew she swam over to get a closer look, with an expression of complete amazement from the buoyant wetness surrounding her! We splashed and played together, delighting in each other's company, and I felt just like the seven year old girl inside me who used to draw horses with heart shaped spots.

When we returned home, Chasta was at the gate to meet us, and Gaela pranced up confidently, surely to share her tales of adventure! It was not until that evening as I sent an email to my dear friend Kathy, thanking her for accompanying us with her beloved horses, that I realized Gaela's christening could not have been in a more appropriate place. We were baptized by immersion in: *Heart Lake!*

Lyrics from one of my favorite songs express how I feel about sweet Gaela:

My funny Valentine,

Sweet comic Valentine,

You make me smile with my heart…

Every day is Valentine's Day

Gaela means "calm healer" in the Gaelic language

Mutual Christening

Photos by Kathy Yaeger

Chapter Fifteen

What is the Nature of Your Emergency?

Our son Evan decided that he enjoyed racing cars so much during his boyhood years that driving as a professional may be his life-path. He was so determined in this vision that he approached us with a plan to attend the local college to complete his high school credits and graduate a year early. He was completely self motivated so recognizing his desire and commitment to his plan and studies, we encouraged him to try, though as a mother who thinks her son is perhaps the world's *most* precious child, racing cars for a living would admittedly not be high on my wish list of choices. In fact, it *horrified* me. Didn't he just want to stay home and play his cello?! Yet we had taught him to reach for the stars with his dreams and had attempted to model that for him so it was time to stand united.

Evan raced against professional Nascar Nextel Cup™ drivers Kasey Kahne and Tony

Stewart as a teenager on two occasions to raise money for their foundations that benefit numerous charities for children and families. Both of these men deserve great admiration for how committed they are to giving back to help others because they are in position to, and more so because they have great hearts. Following Evan's exciting season as a sixteen year old driver with great potential, he was offered an incredible opportunity to travel with Tony Stewart Racing™ as a team member for their pro sprint car tour.

The three of us flew back to Indianapolis, a racing mecca in the United States, on a snowy November day to set him up in housekeeping on his own for the first time at the tender age of seventeen. Then we all returned home for the holidays together as his new season would begin back there at the first of the year so within a short time we began the countdown of the days until he would depart.

It was a strange mixture of excitement and dread for all of us charting our course in unknown territory after being so close as a small family. Recognizing and seizing opportunities in life and making the most of them seemed like a recipe for successful living yet Indianapolis is practically touching the East coast and we lived at sea level on the West. Saying goodbye to family and friends in our small closeknit community was incredibly bittersweet for our tender-hearted son. This job was comparable to 'racing university' in terms of acquiring actual fantastic experience, not to mention the life skills he would acquire living and functioning on his own as a young adult. We kept trying to convince ourselves that this was comparable to going to college out of state or to a foreign exchange student program. "Test the waters" and "go for the adventure" seemed to be a good plan.

"As the days dwindled down to a precious few" as the lyric in a tender old song recorded by Willie Nelson kept playing over in my mind, I could feel my heart beating faster and a lump in my throat most of the time. *God give me strength* was my most fervent prayer. How else could Evan discover if this was truly his heart's desire without trying it---*living* it? If he passed up the opportunity, what would he be thinking in ten years ….? "I wish that I had….?" Or worse yet, "I wish that I could have raced cars professionally but my mother wouldn't let me?" Unless it was illegal or immoral, I would not stand in the way of the young man who means the world to me from living his life to the fullest.

Especially since Chasta had busted me wide open at the seams with her message to *"go for the gusto!"* and to seize the moment along the path of our dreams.

So though I felt as wobbly as Evan that he would be saying goodbye to his world as he knew it for at least a year, I was working hard to come to terms with it, very aware that time was precious and trying to make the most of what we had together. Since his early graduation and his own racing season had come to an end, Evan had been helping his father at our car dealership, engaging his friendly and outgoing personality selling vehicles with good success.

On a night when I was feeling especially tired and vulnerable and had just come home from my parents' home when I had assisted them with personal care needs and was really looking forward to time at home with my husband and son, Gary called to say that their special sale had run late and that they would be staying there overnight. Very disappointed, I reluctantly agreed that it made more sense since they had an early start there in the morning and went outside to say goodnight to the horses. Tossing them a final flake of sweet grass hay for the day, I stopped to savor their rhythmic chewing and contented snorts which soothed my jangled nerves. In between bites, their breath made silvery puffs out in the chilly night air which came in from the always open doors of their stalls, where they would choose to be if I had not come in with dinner. As I stroked their backs and strong hindquarters, I felt how much being near them always helped to take the raw edges off my vulnerability. In spite of all of the countless things on my 'to do' lists, I knew that hanging out with the animals always helps me keep a healthy perspective.

I finally went inside and did only a few of the most significant tasks, then headed for bed and some much needed rest. Knowing these big things were pressing on my mind, I attempted to unwind with deep breathing and Yoga stretching poses and the Tai Chi forms that are becoming so familiar and comforting to me. My nightly ritual is to read (always voraciously and usually about horses) until my eyes feel heavy, go into prayer and meditation and then drift off to sleep. But that night, weary as I felt, sleep did not come. Thoughts of separation from Evan, his safety, Gary's long hours at work, my parent's illnesses and the impending adjustments to it all crowded my frazzled and racing (no pun intended) thoughts.

The minutes ticked by until *finally* I dozed off in the wee hours of the night. By this point, I was sound asleep. Conked out. For any mother who has ever wrestled with menopausal insomnia, the sleep that follows the restlessness is *blessed*. And *deep*.

So there I was, tucked under a heap of blankets in plaid flannel pajamas on this frosty December night, dead to the world, until I was rudely awakened by voices shouting outside my bedroom window. *Loud.* And in *Spanish.* It was so abrupt and sharp that I literally sprang upright in a form of shock that shot me full of adrenaline. Tugging off the fabric eyecovers I wear, I could see it was still dark and glanced at the clock and saw that it was 4 am in the morning. *Arrrrgh!* I had *just* gotten to the deepest level of rest that my body *so* craved when these voices reached a crescendo, apparently just below me.

Why hadn't I learned to speak Spanish?! It was certainly on my list of life ambitions. I knew some rudimentary French from high school but ours is a community where many residents have Hispanic roots. It would be such help to children and their families when I volunteered at the local schools. This conversation that I could hear blaring under my window sounded like an argument and one that seemed to be heating up. If only I had developed my language skills, facilitation of whatever the conflict was would be so much easier to resolve.

As my heart raced, I wondered if maybe the voices were coming from the television, tucked in a cabinet on the floor below me. But why in the world would Evan be watching TV at 4 am? He enjoyed his Spanish classes at school but had never been so diligent as to watch television in a foreign language.

Suddenly it hit me like a bolt of lightening that *Evan was not home. Nor Gary.* And the voices continued, seeming to increase in volume while I realized that something was very wrong with this picture.

Oh, God. Why weren't our dogs barking? Where were the voices coming from? Were they on TV? Was someone *stealing* the TV? Had they silenced the dogs? Should I go investigate? Was I having an emergency situation? *Duh?!*

As quietly as I could, I reached for the telephone, dialing 911 for the first time as a homeowner/taxpayer in all my years. An alert voice answered immediately, *"What is the nature of your emergency?"* "Hello", I whispered, telling the dispatcher my name. "I'm not sure what is happening, but I just awoke to extremely loud voices that appear to be having a conflict and they are speaking Spanish, which I do not understand. My husband and son are away and none of my three dogs are responding by barking which they always do. I cannot tell if it is the television or if someone is inside or outside of my home!" She replied by asking me if I had a place where I could lock myself into. "Yes," I continued, "the bathroom inside this room locks." *"Good,"* the operator responded, "go inside quietly and take the phone with you and stay on the line." "Uh, I can't---the phone here is not a cellular one that I can remove" I said and she returned with, "OK, then leave it there off the hook and go lock yourself in the bathroom—I am sending the sheriff immediately—how do I tell him to get inside?"

Giving her the instructions, I tiptoed into the bathroom and hunkered down on the lid of the toilet seat, wondering why I bothered being so quiet with the blaring noise. Attempting to take deep calming breaths I repeated prayers that would help me to relax and trust the mighty shield of God, tripping over my tongue as I tried to recite the 23rd Psalm from memory. As my muscles began to soften, my closed eyes helped me to tap into the stillness within.

Until suddenly the loud voices began to speak in *English* in what was obviously a newscast about a series of gang slayings. Oh *great*. It *was* the TV! And *who* was changing the channels?! If *'they'* were planning to steal it, why not just get on with it?! Suddenly the realization that an intruder(s) was indeed in our house erased my efforts at relaxation. It suddenly seemed reasonable to go out the window onto the roof of our veranda porch and get safely to one of my neighbors across the acreage.

So picture this: a silver haired form in a chenille robe and moccasins climbing out the window and inching along the frosty cedar shakes and then what? Leap off the roof onto the frozen grass? There is a large arbor behind the back door---maybe I could crawl onto that and somehow slide down the posts, firehouse style, hoping not to snag my robe or skin my knees on the rose thorns. But that would be in full view of the room where the television was. And the gang of thieves. And what ever happened to following the dispatcher's instructions to stay locked in the bathroom? Thoughts of my sweet dogs being hurt gave rise to new boldness but I realized that my plan was not only ridiculous but totally unsafe as I moved slowly along the slippery shingles looking for anything stationery to hold onto.

Suddenly lights beamed from the end of our long driveway and a sedan rolled up slowly. Was it the sheriff? Or reinforcements to drive the getaway car? Blessedly, I heard the radio crackle as he stepped out of the car and realized that help had arrived. Filled with new courage, I inched back to the window, crawled inside and moved along the wall of the hallway to a another window facing his car to the outside which I cracked and watched the sheriff approach the entrance that I had told him how to get into. *"Officer?"* I croaked. *"Connie?!"* he replied, *"Are you all right?"* "Yes," I nodded. "Stay there, I will be right in," he said, finishing our conversation in hushed tones.

Suddenly realizing that he was taking his life in his hands just walking through the garage where heaps of recyclables may fall on him simply trying to navigate in the darkness to the inner door, I sheepishly waited for this kind stranger to help me. All sounds seemed amplified. The TV blaring, his footsteps crunching the gravel in his regulation boots, my own breathing. The beam from his light was enormous and completely lit up the entry as my renewed courage took me to the stair landing to watch. Within a few minutes, it became perfectly quiet but for his kind voice. *"Connie, you are safe and can come down now."*

Entering the room to survey the scene with wide eyes, I looked over to where the officer stood next to our golden retriever, Donny, who was alive and well and swishing his tail happily. *"I think I found the culprit,"* the sheriff started to explain with the corners of his mouth turned up. "He was sound asleep on top of the television remote" pointing to the dog next to him who had just become his new best friend. "It's still warm and has dog hair on it," he couldn't resist telling me as he held it up in his hand.

Donny has his own rug and knows perfectly well the sofa is off limits. I looked over to see that our sixteen year old black lab, Hootie, was still completely conked out in front of the fireplace, sound asleep through all of it. By now, our Jack Russell terrier, Cosmo, had awakened and appeared to see what he was missing, his tiny tail moving his entire hind-quarters off the ground in rapid movements. *Guard dogs, indeed!*

"Oh, my, *I feel so foolish!* I truly apologize for calling-----it just never occurred to me......"
I tried to sound articulate under the ridiculous circumstances. "No problem — you did the right thing" he replied. We actually like false alarms as much as you do. We wish they all were."

I looked at his name tag and asked him if he was related to a prominent local judge. "My father," he smiled. "My father designed your father's law offices years ago" I told him. "Are you related to Gary Funk?" he continued. "My husband" came my reply. *"Small world"* we said in unison.

At that strange point of sensation where your adrenaline rush is reversed by the chemistry of blessed relief, I heard another noise outside on the veranda porch which turned out to be a female officer, apparent backup for the hardened canine criminal who by now was wagging his tail furiously, eager for a wee hours party. As he bounded in to greet the newest visitor, his tail smacked an antique crystal vase which shattered on the tile floor of the dining room, distributing razor sharp shards all over the crime scene. All this while Hootie snored blissfully and Cosmo ran in tight circles. When the female officer heard the report, she was as good a sport as her partner in keeping her laughter in check. She reassured me that I could have *potentially* been in danger and it is "always better to be safe than sorry."

After they left, the dogs resumed their sleeping positions while I stood there sweeping up the broken glass, shot full of adrenaline, now tinged with embarrassment. Since I would not be able to return to sleep all jived up at that point, I had time to think about the operator's question, "What is the nature of your emergency?"

Webster's defines an emergency as: a sudden generally unexpected occurrence demanding immediate attention.

It made me think of the horses. How for them any sudden unexpected occurrence demands their attention. That is the way they are wired---some more than others. It is how they have survived as a species so magnificently. And yet, as we become their partners in domestic life, how it is our *responsibility* to help them to discern that almost *all* of life is not a true emergency---or that actually *very little* truly is. If humans provide strong leadership, as their lead horse would in the wild, domestic horses learn to remain calm and not react in a flight or fight response to every sudden sound or motion.

But how often in life do we as humans *create* the dramas that become emergencies and how easily can that become a pattern? Even an addictive one. We all know someone who can conjure up a crisis if life gets dull even for a moment. Reactivity can become a way of life. Headlines trumpet these one after another. Tabloids announce emergency relational conflicts galore. As a society, we have been programmed for the other shoe to drop. *Hard.* And we create what we focus on and give our attention to, even if we are innocently sneaking a peak at the dreadful headlines in the aisle at the supermarket.

True lead horses in a wild herd are great role models. This mare is supremely intelligent and wastes no energy looking for trouble or sweating the small stuff. She is extra vigilant and aware, but incredibly calm and confident. She saves her big responses for a true life and death situation and conserves her resources for the sake of the herd---her family---the community.

So how could our personal lives be different if we lived in that state of calm, confident awareness? If Gary and Evan had been home or the dogs awake and with me, I might have been braver. And I *in no way* want to discount how devastating a violation an actual robbery is for victims. Or label *any* group of people as possible perpetrators. But what did I learn from this situation besides keeping the remote off the sofa---not to mention the dogs?

That almost all of life is *not* an emergency. *Thank God.* That much of my choice making can contribute to the consistent manageability and comfort of my days---and nights! That I do not have to allow the chronic drama of the self created emergencies of others to affect my inner peace. In my neighborhood or around the world. *That I could have chosen to sleep through the whole thing like dear old Hootie.*

And that I *do* want to learn to speak Spanish and get to know my neighbors better and help the kids at school who are new to the community and are learning a different language. Maybe I will get some tapes to listen to before I fall asleep….

And I also need to drop off a box of fresh donuts at the sheriff's office.

Cosmo, small in stature only!

Don Diego, Keeper of the Peace

Chapter Sixteen

Horse Sense

The noble minds, majestic spirits and wondrously agile bodies of horses have been woven into the tapestry of every geography and culture since their creation. And up until a hundred years ago when motors came on the scene, they were a part of most every family as partners for transportation and cultivation. So it is little wonder that references to them permeate our language and it is my tender hope that they always will.

In researching many cultures, one will find common idiomatic expressions relating to horses that express wisdom, humor and practical advice. If we are *saddled* with something, it is a burden to bear. This has long been a part of our speech and yet it has not been until recent years that humans have really considered the value of proper saddle fit as being an incredibly important consideration to the health of the horse and that they could actually be a burden to the one made to wear them. I believe that everyone who has the privilege to be entrusted with the guardianship of any equine or simply loves horses should witness firsthand the *remarkable* documentary film created by Stormy May called *The Path of the Horse*. Like the other amazing humans featured on her film, Stormy sees horses as wise and feeling sentient beings ---highly evolved mammals like humans with a wide range of emotions. The beautiful and emotionally evocative art of artist, writer and visionary Kim McElroy is included because that is precisely how Kim portrays the Equine species, helping others to see through the eyes of their heart. The message that Stormy and Kim and those featured is so provocative and important and challenges us as a species to receive the subtle yet powerful communications that our own horses offer us and horses as a whole are presenting as gifts. Stormy possesses tremendous courage to share her journey and message and is a key piece of the vast puzzle of increasing consciousness that will enhance *all* relationships. Watch her website as she continues to pursue the passion that propels her forward.

Which leads us to *horseplay*, something the species Equus operates on efficiently and effectively, sometimes quietly or by *kicking up a lot of dust.* It's not that they don't take life or each other seriously, rather that they have a language that is playful at heart and one humans could excel at too, if we had the mindset to do so. Picture a family reunion where everyone brings something to the table, literally, and then after enjoying what each has to offer, congregates in an open field and plays touch football. The human family at its best. Horses know how to keep this playful spirit as a way of being.

They *hit the ground running* at birth and never stop the forward motion that ensures survival. Only when humans confine them to an extreme is their movement suspended. *Hitting the ground running* applied to humans connotes plunging into a project at full speed and being prepared in advance for what could happen, which is positively horselike.

We have been warned not to *change horses in the middle of the stream*. Anyone who has ever ridden a horse through water knows that it requires focused attention to safety and footing. Best to complete the task at hand before starting another one. Good advice.

Hold your horses and *Whoa!* as admonitions to slow down and stop by coming to a halt are so pervasive in Western culture that they have become universal expressions and with the frenetic pace of our modern lives that seems faster than the planet can spin, they seem like an excellent idea. Take the time to slow down long enough to smell the roses, stop for a cup of lemonade from a child's stand or to notice a spectacular sunset. In developing relationships with my horses, *Whoa* has become a very special place for us. A time out. Finding *Whoa* together means time to rest, exhale. *Relax.* What could you do to add more *Whoa* time into your day? I have begun writing it prominently on my too full calendar schedule. Just seeing the word makes me slow down and feel the corners of my mouth turn up!

And if we hit a snag along the way and are besieged by the setbacks that punctuate every life, what a great feeling to regain your momentum so that you are *back in the saddle again*. We feel our resiliency after losing a job when we find one that we like better or recover our bearings after a relationship ends and we risk starting anew. Getting *back in the saddle* can represent the courage to face a devastating illness with the determination and hope to heal and recover. We find our inner resources atop that shiny leather metaphor for moving on. We realize our inner pluck.

And by taking the time to discover and develop who we are physically, mentally, emotionally and spiritually, we come into our wholeness. And using our equine friends as a model again, become as *healthy as a horse.* Rarely is a horse like a hothouse flower. Instead they possess a vigor that is hearty, strong and adaptable.

There isn't much point to *locking the stable door after the horse has bolted.* By then it is probably too late! So that expression could teach us to live in a greater level of awareness. Think in a proactive way. Prevent operator error. Trust God, but close the gate. Much like the wise Muslim expression, *Trust Allah, but tie up your camel.* The divine and human in concert. And if our hearts are true and just and our animals considered brethren, our horses and camels will remain willingly and quietly with us, tied or otherwise.

And the *horse of a different color?* Why not? We live in a world that has joyously begun to celebrate the beauty in diversity and what makes us different from each other. One of the most riveting and hopeful books that I have ever read written by David Oliver Relin called *Three Cups of Tea*, tells the true story of Greg Mortenson, a mountaineer who lived among the people of Pakistan who saved his life after losing his way on an expedition in their incredibly rugged and unforgiving terrain. He was so touched by their kindness and moved by the poverty and lack of formal education that he pledged to come back and build schools for *all* children regardless of gender, in a culture that had not formally provided education for girls. What is so moving about this real life adventure is that he did not attempt to change or convert them to his way of thinking, but to encourage and support them in their own culture and offer the gift of knowledge which can overpower despair. He gave them, along with his many supporters and foundation, *The Central Asian Institute*, the *tangible hope* which education can offer. Real tools for personal and regional empowerment. The success, though fraught with the ongoing challenges of a war-torn area, expanded into Afghanistan.

How can we open ourselves to life by seeing what is on the other side of the fence or the planet and inviting something and someone new into our lives? Especially when it can make the difference between life and death for people of all nations and faith traditions. Often the lives of those most vulnerable, the innocent civilians who are going about their daily lives with kindness and respect toward each other. David Oliver Relin's eloquent account of the personal and passionate mission of Greg Mortenson and his dedicated supporters is one of the most important stories of our times and illustrates what we need, as a universal culture, to focus our attention and energy and resources on: empowering *all* through books rather than bombs, since true power comes from acceptance of self and others and the confidence that education and understanding can bring—that we are ultimately one human family, interdependent with all life forms that we must preserve and protect.

Though the list of horse related expressions is long enough to be cliché, I could *cut to the chase,* and by doing so, get to the heart of the matter. That is where horses are true experts. They possess *horse sense.* Sound, practical judgment based on finely tuned instinctive responses. And their large and forgiving hearts. A curiosity about life and a willingness to celebrate it by kicking up their heels on a regular basis. Uncommonly common sense. Listed under synonyms in the thesaurus for the phrase common sense, the sister to *horse sense,* is the wonderful word, gumption.

Got gumption?

Chasta and Gaela enjoy their Easter carrot hunt at liberty

Three mares with plenty of gumption!

Photo by John Yaeger

Chapter Seventeen

The Grass is Always Greener
on the other Side of the Fence

Chad, The Wonder Horse

Thinking the grass is always greener on the other side of the fence can really be a difficult obstacle to overcome in life because the belief is so pervasive in our society yet it is actually a mistaken notion, a myth, or an actual lie... *Unless it's true.*

Like in the spring of the first year that we had

our beloved horse, Chad, when he munched his pasture down to nubs and the neighbors across the fenceline had yet to pull out their lawnmower for the season. The grass was not only *greener* on the other side of the fence, but longer, more lush and full of his favorite sweet clover.

So, clever boy that he was, he took the wooden doweled gate latch in his teeth and wiggled it loose until he could let himself out, mosey down our long driveway, out onto the road and over to the sweet spring splendor of their grass.

Returning home from running errands in my car, I noticed him over there as I pulled up, free as a bird. Nothing mischievous about it. Simply a matter of a better meal. And how *handy* to be so close by! As I went to get a halter and lead rope to retrieve him, he was already heading over to greet me, knowing that we had given him our hearts (and lots of carrots!) as I assured him that we would go to our own longer grass on another pasture.

Which settled things temporarily until he ate his fill at home, and being a supremely intelligent horse, headed over beyond the fenceline like an escape artist where the pickins were better. Chad's behavior was simply horselike, since they are designed to forage for the best food available. When ours was eaten, it was his nature to move on. I could provide him all the best extra grass hay in the world, but if there was *fresh* green grass nearby that he could see and smell, that is what he preferred and was more than happy to accommodate himself. This led me to taking him for frequent trips to verdant grassy places in our nearby woods to satisfy his appetite.

But what of humans who can be so preoccupied with what they think is a better deal that someone else has? Do we want what the Jones' have, and do we think that is what will make us happy? Or like women who are voluptuous envying my flat chest and vice versa since the only cleavage that I have ever had is between my toes and when I was a nursing mother, and that was short lived and then right back to being able to wear my blouses backwards. And those of us with fair complexions and hazel eyes wishing for olive skin and dark ones. Hair stylists tell me that practically no one comes in thinking that they have fabulous hair and want them to change it. Do we covet our neighbor's husband because he cleans the gutters regularly only to find out that he also has anger management issues? We humans often think that others have closer families, blondes have more fun and strangers have happier and more fulfilling lives.

And sometimes it is just a matter of not having enough information. Like people who think that they would love to sell everything and retire to the country and open a bed and breakfast inn. Perfect---romantic, blissful and exciting! And in many ways, it is, but also a tremendous amount of dedicated hard work. It may suit a person/couple perfectly or drive them totally bonkers. I've always wanted to…. start an antiques business, open a restaurant, sell real estate---whatever. *Try it! No one should hold themselves back from following a dream!* I was totally inspired by Martha Beck's books, *Finding Your Own North Star* and *Steering by Starlight.* She is a bright, laugh out loud---make that *howl*---writer who gives wise and practical advice on living your best life. So check out what you are dreaming of—it may be right up your alley.

That is what our son Evan thought about racing cars. He loved it so much that when the opportunity came up to move back East and work for one of his racing heroes, the iconic Tony Stewart, he thought he would follow his dream and work his way up the ladder to become a professional driver. Until he realized that he loved to *race,* but wasn't too crazy about the all consuming racing *life-style*. In fact, it did not suit him at all. Born and raised in the Pacific Northwest where there is only hobby racing, he knew that the way to go pro was to be where the racers and tracks are and he thought he was ready and that he knew what it would be like. Until he *lived* it. Seven long days a week working on race cars, traveling to the next track and racing into the wee hours of the nights. Eating in restaurants. Sleeping in hotels. For a *minimum* of nine months of the year. Often longer.

People can adjust to any kind of a schedule, but it has to be in your nature to *love* being on the road to enjoy this lifestyle. As much as Evan enjoys racing, he felt that it was too singular an ambition and that he would have to sacrifice all else that is important to him to attain success as a racer and that the costs to his personal life would be too high. *Evan is still racing for his dreams,* he has just decided not to pursue them in the fast lane of an oval track.

Yet what a gift at eighteen years of age to have given it his best effort by taking the opportunity to test the waters. It was a wonderful and very challenging year of self discovery and gave him the time to ask himself, "What *do* I want to see/feel/accomplish in life? What *are* my talents and desires?"

And they may change. The most interesting people that I know are the ones who have had a rich and varied life in terms of experiences. If young people ever ask for my advice, I always tell them to follow their hearts, travel, and try lots of jobs and experiences. Join the Peace Corps. Go on a mission trip. Learn a foreign language. Visit a monastery. Work in a sustainable organic chocolate factory. Go build kites and fly them. Sign up for a wide variety of classes and workshops. Study what *fascinates* you.

And it is never too late to discover what our deepest yearnings as humans truly are. Sometimes it is just a matter of asking ourselves some important questions. Like: What am I afraid of? What excites me? What brings me happiness? Peace? Fulfillment? What is God *calling* me to be? What would I do if I knew that I could not fail? And maybe more importantly, what *is* failure?

Give it a try! There really are no failures — only lack of attempts. What is the worst that could happen? You can always change your mind. The distinguished poet, Naomi Shabib Nye wrote: *"You can fall like a leaf at any moment and then decide what to do with your life."*

Should you have a horse? Of your very own? Now *that* is one dream that many of us have had long held romantic notions of since childhood. *I* certainly did. And it should not be entered into lightly. It is not for the faint of heart. Horses are living, breathing *amazing* creatures, who although tamable, retain their wild nature forever. When well cared for, they live a long time and require considerable amounts of attention, education and financial commitment.

I have found that having a horse is very much like having a child. Children are tamable, too, (sort of) and if you have done your job well, they will also retain their wild nature at heart. They both challenge you, confuse you, and confine you. Yet bring you so much joy and sheer delight that enables you to live in Heaven on Earth. You cannot remember life before them or imagine it without them. Though you felt whole and complete before their presence in your world, they give you a reason to get up in the morning and bless your days with exciting discoveries forever-more.

Because knowing and loving a child and a horse is knowing and loving yourself. It is the best way that I know to have everything that you always wanted within the fenceline of *you*, because God always produces a bumper crop when His seed falls on fertile soil.

And when you know and love yourself, the grass is always green.

Chad and Hooter in the early days.
They are together again eternally where the grass is always greener...

PART III

Like Rings on a Tree

Growth is an Inside Job

Chapter Eighteen

Small Things with Great Love

People say the strangest things at class re-
unions. During the gathering for the twenty
fifth anniversary of my graduation from the
small island town where I attended high
school, a boy (now an aging half bald man)
who I barely knew as a classmate strode up to
me purposefully and looked dumbfounded
and profoundly disappointed. The fact that
he was deep into his cocktails apparently relieved him of any inhibitions he may have
had with his feelings that night and without
even exchanging greetings, he launched into
his impulsive expression: *"Man,* I thought
You were going to do something *big!!!"*

Somewhat taken aback, I replied with a tone
as pleasant as I could muster with his whis-
key breath in my face, "What do you mean?"
"Well," he went on, slurring his words, "of *all*
people I thought *you* would *be* somebody---
do something, *you know?!"* he said resolutely
as he surveyed me up and down warily.

Apparently he had read my little bio that attendees were asked to include. Mine was something like: "went to college, got married to my first love, collect antiques, practiced dental hygiene until our child was born, adore my son Evan, love to read and write and spend time in nature with animals…"

In other words, I was 'still in the valley' close to the islands and not out maybe saving the world? Did he think that my name would be in lights and have my star on Celebrity Row or discover a cure for cancer? I wasn't sure exactly *where* he was coming from and had to look on the tag on his chest to even remember his name.

Was he relieved to perceive through his own filter someone who he thought would 'succeed' in the great big world had fumbled her life as much as he thought he had with his own? Or did he wish that I could have had huge recognition so that he could cheer me on from the sidelines thinking his photo would be next to mine when my high school annual was published in *People Magazine?*

Politely telling him that my life was richly blessed and that I wished the same for him and excusing myself to walk away, I left him shaking his head in thinly veiled disgust.

Somehow his remarks popped into my consciousness as I mailed copies of my first book to family, friends, and even some customers! Did I think that having a book in print with an independent publisher counted as finally doing something *big* or that it changed me into *somebody?* Hardly! But the timing was incredibly serendipitous and laden with the synchronicities that I have grown accustomed to experiencing living my life with purpose to the fullest.

My books arrived on the same day at the same time as greeting cards that I had printed from a separate source featuring my grandmother riding an enormous pig at the ranch where she grew up. She had given me the photograph nearly twenty years previously and I loved it so much that my first response was to tell her that I would have it made into a card. "What do you mean?" she queried. "Greeting cards, Nanny," I said, using our family name for my maternal grandmother. "People would *love* them! This photograph epitomizes the pioneer spirit that makes you so special!" She smiled and shook her head, but seemed, as *she* would have said, "tickled" by the thought.

After I had a website created by the talented Davina Andrée of Arrowhead Graphics it seemed natural to finally have cards printed from my vast collections of copyright free antique art and photographs. The cards arrived on a day in June that would have been my grandmother's 96th birthday when the gorgeous peonies in my gardens that were from starts that she had given me were in full bloom.

Cutting a gloriously fragrant feathery fuchsia colored bunch, I took them to the nearby hospital where my mother laid in critical care following surgery after a prolonged illness. Heavily sedated and on life support, I told Mom of the arrival of the books and cards and held up the photo close to her face and shared that I would also take peonies to Nanny's grave in her stead and share my story. She strained to look at the picture as she listened closely. "Someone may order this from halfway around the world to give to someone they love because they are inspired and delighted by it," I assured her. The quote inside the card reads *Life is either a grand adventure or nothing at all"* which is attributed to Helen Keller, a woman with a triumphant spirit who inspired people the world over. My grandmother, born in the same era with a birthday two days apart, was named Helen Sellers.

"What do you think of *that,* Mom?" I asked softly. "It's *good,* I like it" she said in a whisper, deeply aware and touched in spite of being hooked up to a morphine drip. "And so would Nanny," I offered. *"Yes,"* she smiled weakly, "She *would."*

So there I was at the post office ready to mail the books as the line moved slowly and friends and neighbors all stopped to ask how my parents were getting along. My next stop was the bank where I received the same loving support. As I stepped outside the door of the bank, a squirrel scooted up to me expectantly and stood unusually quiet, just a few swishes of his tail but looking up alertly. "Hey, little fellow, I wish I had a treat for you" I had just stated when the door opened behind me and the teller who had just shared comforting words as she assisted me with my transaction leaned down and said *"Hey Guido, here are your peanuts!"* A perfect gentleman, the squirrel reached up and took the booty, gave her a thankful look with his eyes, turned and scurried off. "Oh, that was *Gus,"* she smiled, "He only takes one at a time. Guido grabs two and sticks them in his mouth like little tusks! If I don't watch for him, he presses himself up against the glass door in distress!"

I could sense myself feeling lighter observing this delightful exchange and special relationship as I headed for the business office of the lovely woman who typed my manuscript and supported me through out the process. Marella, with her vast experience, also offered me words of encouragement as we recalled the fun we had shared and what we were learning together.

My next stop was to see my friend Kate who operates a local photo processing shop. She had developed and scanned the book photos and helped me in innumerable ways. Because news travels fast in our small town, she had heard about my mother's situation and had given her a priceless gift---a Teddy bear named "Stitches" that her sister had given her years ago when she had a similar surgery in this life and death situation. She felt it was my mother's time to hug the bear whenever she felt pain as she recovered to remind her how precious life is.

As I thanked her for the beautiful gesture and all she had done to help me, I gave her a copy of 'our' book. One of my neighbors who farms the valley here on Pleasant Ridge came in. Her horse crazy granddaughters have spent days here with our horses and one in particular has helped me numerous times with field trips for local schoolchildren. The day before I had stopped at their berry stand run entirely by the grandchildren and commented that the kids gave me excellent service and always helped me to choose the most sumptuous strawberries possible. I grow berries at home, but cannot resist those kids *or* their product when I drive by! Their grandmother smiled to think of her darling clan.

As she left, Kate and I walked out into the doorway of her shop to savor the long awaited sunshine of summer after a rainy gray spring. Breaking our reverie was the screeching siren of a local fire truck that sped toward us, driven by two young volunteers who had answered an emergency call to assist paramedics in taking my mother to the hospital several days before that and my father following a stroke a mere five weeks previously. Both of these twenty something men were registered for Kindergarten by my mother when she had been the local elementary school secretary and was there throughout their education until cheering them on to graduation.

I said a silent prayer for whoever they were going to help and realized again with gratitude how they played an important role in saving my mother's life and had been an enormous comfort to all of us.

Heading for my husband's truck, I jumped in and turned the key. The message on the dash lit up to tell me that the fuel was low and the air pressure was down in the left rear tire. Stopping a few blocks down the street at a small locally owned gas station by a couple who have delighted the entire valley with their performances in community theatre, I filled the tank. Going inside to sign my receipt, I saw two familiar smiling faces of the employees that run the store for the owners. We quipped (trying to make an awful thing for everyone bearable) about the fact that the $104.07 total for the gas used to be the price of the *truck*. The two of them were just changing shifts and in order for him to go back and help me fill my tire, she had to stay over to watch the till and I thought about how her children had gone to school with my son and how my mother had tended to all of their needs over the years as their school secretary.

Driving off with a full tank and firm tires, I marveled at the gifts of living in this small rural community---this valley—and felt I was *exactly* where I needed to be. Heading to the recycle center with a full truckload,

I thought about how much I missed Evan now that he was grown and on his own, since recycling has always been a ritual that he helped me with that we enjoyed doing together as stewards of our amazing planet.

I felt profoundly grateful that it was not my calling to do something *big* or to *be somebody*, but rather to make my contributions in small but meaningful ways whenever and wherever I could with the gifts that I have been given. My book was merely a larger manifestation of what I had attempted to do over the years sharing stories and making connections. Trying to encourage others as they have done for me.

Mother Teresa said, *"We cannot do great things, only small things with great love."* So that was what I realized when my classmate's words, "I thought you would do something *big*" rang back into my ears.

I have been *loving big* in the best way that I knew how in each stage of my development. Not always very well and often quite messy but *big*. With enthusiasm and sincerity. I hope and pray mostly with accountability and humility for the countless mistakes that I have made along the way. If I have been able to succeed at all doing small things with great love, it is because of the examples set for me by my mother, Kay, and her mother, Helen, who epitomized this way of being in the world.

As I laid in bed at night praying that God would give me the strength to debut my book at an equine event to benefit horses and women in need called *Celebrate the Horse* with my mother still recovering, I knew that I was representing all women and horses and that is what my mother and grandmother would want me to do.

My Mother and Grandmother were so strong on my mind last spring on a road trip when I took Chasta and Gaela to visit the spectacular beauty of Gateway 2 Ranch in British Columbia, Canada, which belongs to friends Kevin and Liz Mitten Ryan. They provided my horses with a lovely ten acre paddock complete with its own lake and I had dreamed of releasing them on the entire 320 acres which is about what a wild herd would claim and what her horses enjoy on a daily basis. As dramatic as it sounds, I had a deep desire to release my horses to that level of freedom, something that most domestic horses have never had the privilege of ex-periencing in any way. Being on that moun-taintop made me feel larger than life, almost surreal, like being in a movie, only in perfect present time. Knowing that the worst case scenario of allowing my mares to run would mean that I would have to find them at the end of the week, deep down I knew they would likely enjoy their exploration and come right back to their base camp to see me. Truly, I did not feel as if I were 'testing' the bond of our relationship, rather it felt like a once in a lifetime gift that I could offer them by being in that sacred place and something that I have always dreamed of doing.

So together we enjoyed a trek to the summit walking on the ground on line and when we reached the top, I drew them both close to me, petting them behind their ears and down their withers, in total awe of the panoramic view of unspoiled natural beauty surrounding us. Silently, I asked Chasta to run for every horse who has ever been confined, neglected and abused. For all the PMU mares hooked to constant catheters. For every soul who has ever been oppressed. It was *so* important to me for her to know that what I wanted the most was freedom for her spirit as well as for her body. And for Gaela as well. She looked directly into my eyes for a long time as I undid her rope halter, then turned and galloped down the mountain. Releasing Gaela in a cloud of dust, I felt a surge of my own freedom as they disappeared over the rise below. Though I had my camera poised, it was such a magnificent moment that the only lens that recorded it was in my own eyes and heart. When we finally returned to the paddocks below, there they were, waiting, and it felt *incredible* to know our relationship was a choice.

I can not heal *for* Chasta or Gaela or the PMU mares or their foals or women, men and children in foreign countries or my Mother and Grandmother or wounded soldiers of all nations. Yet I can heal *with* them all.

If I go back to another class reunion and the committee requires a bio, I think that I will simply write the quote by Mother Teresa and leave it at that. And I will continue to feel grateful for and celebrate the fact that I am *Holy as Thou*.

My grandmother's wisdom for living was:

**"Use it up, wear it out,
make do or do without."**

*My Grandmother, Helen Sellers, on her child-
hood ranch. Apparently her older
brothers got the horses...*

*"Life is either a grand adventure
or nothing at all."*

Helen Keller

Chapter Nineteen

Interspecies Communication: Chasta as Midwife

Communication *fascinates* me. Information being sent and received. And returned. Feedback exchanged. As much as high speed communication along the information highway advances our abilities to learn, it is my fervent prayer that the children of today are still talking to each other through cans and string. And listening to the roar of the ocean by putting shells up to their ears. Because in the case of a shell, a magical smile on the face of a child is feedback, indeed.

When we were growing up, my sister Debbie and I would wait to hear our parents retiring to the family room to watch TV (the biggest laughs usually came during *The Jackie Gleason Show* and it was torture to be able to hear the clinking of spoons against their dishes which meant they were enjoying ice cream without us again) when one of us would sneak the vacuum cleaner hose out of the hall closet which was our ticket to keep talking and giggling long into the night between our bunk beds without fear of discovery. What's a little filth up against your mouth and ears when you can hear that wonderful, wacky echo reverberating through the tube shaped receiver?

And walkie talkies. In their early years my brother and cousins were sure they were spies, especially when it came to keeping secrets from the girls. One of our methods of communication was to shout or drop notes down a laundry chute that was under a wooden lid outside my cousin Lorean's bedroom. And since it was perfectly reasonable for young spies to congregate in the basement laundry room to debrief, they often received our messages in hushed tones that reverberated back up into her cavernous walk-in closet. It seems like they often spoke in codes that bonded them to the secrecy of a shared language. And the fact that our father had been a radio officer in his youth when in the US Navy who received and translated Morse code and lived to tell the tales was an obvious inspiration.

While the young male spies were plotting their latest espionage, we female cousins were settling in for our slumber party in Lorean's bedroom that seemed to me to be created for a princess. She had a white four poster canopied bed with pink ruffles everywhere and I have incredible memories of being tucked in between Lorean and Debbie as we pretended to be horses and combed each others' manes for what felt like hours. Although we chattered and giggled constantly, the feelings needed no words and visions of ponies and unicorns danced in our heads as the lights went out and the sleepy spies bunked together down the hall in the stately old English Tudor home of my favorite extended family members.

Horses are teaching me daily to be aware of the fact that *everything means something* and that *most* of communication is non-verbal. A wonderful resource written by Marshall Rosenberg, Ph.D. called *Nonviolent Comunication : A Language of Life* is really helping me to focus on empathic listening and observation without judgment. So I often think about communing with nature and the heightened sense of receptivity it creates, and if I feel intrigued by communication with my *own* species, imagine how I enjoy the possibilities with another! And the joy I experience observing the animals that make their homes with us sharing relationships with each other.

We have had a mated pair of wild Canadian Geese return to our pond year after year in the spring and they enjoy co-habitating with our domestic ducks and are tame enough to allow us to savor time watching them while they eat the grain we provide.

Last season a second pair landed in a nearby pasture and looked around at the real estate. They apparently liked what they saw and headed for the waters' edge, when pair number one, the regulars, intervened. *What a racket!* There was a chorus of honking like what you might hear in urban rush hour traffic as our resident male and female drove them back through a rail fence. The discussion, still heated, continued until they flew skyward, honking all the way as they promised, *"We'll be back!"* Returning for the next three days, they renewed their efforts and either our couple was worn down by attrition or decided they liked the newcomers once they got to know them. We now had two pairs communing on a common pond. Imagine my surprise a week later when I looked down to see sixteen total geese in various positions around the wind rippled water, some searching for insects, others enjoying a relaxing swim and most stretched out in the sunshine taking siestas. There goes the neighborhood!

As usual, Chasta was taking it all in and looking to see if I was, too. She is the commander in chief of the resident animal population here, wild and domestic. I am not sure if it was a democratic process or if she was self-appointed. Nevertheless, she seemed as eager as we were for our final pair of feed store ducks to hatch ducklings.

A year before our other female duck had laid sixteen perfect eggs on an elaborate nest in an old tool box in the garden and Chasta had brought it to my attention by hanging her head over the fence and whinnying to me. It took me *days* to interpret her communication, which then became totally obvious in hindsight. Chasta seemed as devastated as we were when one morning I discovered Mama Duck (or what little remained of her) dead and her eggs broken and scattered. It was too cold and wet to attempt to save the few that were left intact after being ripped brutally from under the belly of their mother. Chasta surely witnessed the violation and must have felt powerless to help her over the fenceline. She stood and hung her head listlessly in that spot for days.

So last spring I came down to the pond with a doghouse riding in a wheelbarrow and announced to Chasta and Gaela that it was a nesting place for Georgia, our female duck. Our neighbor Nonie and I gathered appropriate bedding materials to help her get started and scattered them nearby and I filled the inside of the arched doorway with grain. Chasta and Gaela, happy as they were with the company of the ducks, loved the added bonus access to corn, even if it was intended to be off limits. Especially for Chasta who has a huge attraction for the forbidden. Where was my video camera when each of them took a turn at straddling the doghouse and sticking their heads into the too small opening upside down and backwards in an attempt to reach the coveted grain?

It wasn't long before a lovely nest was built inside lined with horsehair shed from springtime grooming sessions. Then eight gorgeous eggs appeared. We were back in business!

Until one day when I saw a bedraggled Georgia making tight circles in the pond, fast and furious, with her mate, Frank, swimming frantically behind her. Looking up, I saw the eggs, broken and obviously raided! *Poor Georgia!*

So I loaded the doghouse on the wheelbarrow and scoured it completely and set about creating a safe new place to put it near the pond where I could keep a closer eye on her. Chasta seemed bereft when she saw Georgia and I wondered if she had been in the same pasture as her duck friends when the intruder came whether she could have prevented it and protected Georgia. Frank was very attentive but there was only one of him. They needed *community.*

So I started leaving the horses on that pasture regularly to see if it would make a difference and we would soon see a new nest and another group of eggs. And that is when the Canadian geese arrived with their friends. And *their* friends. As gracious as Frank and Georgia were as hosts, all that company must have worn thin because the nest remained empty and Georgia kept disappearing for days at a time. When I *did* see her at feeding time, she seemed disheveled and scrawny. Finally I stopped seeing her altogether.

My mother's health was in a severe decline and when I walked through the pasture on my way to visit her down the road, I called to Georgia regularly, hoping the familiar sound of my voice would cause her to reveal her hidden location. Nonie advised me kindly to let go of my desires for the season---it was too late in the year for baby ducks. With a heavy heart, I told Frank we would look for another friend for him as soon as we could.

As captivated as I am about my relationships with our animals and all of nature, I still have *much* work (and a lot of play!) to do regarding my perceptions. People often ask me if I am a "horse whisperer" because they have heard the popular term. I usually tell them that my relationships are all about careful observations and listening with awareness and attempting to experience the elusive *feel*. Lest I *ever* get too smug in my assessment of my levels of awareness, Chasta constantly provides me with experiences to expand my horizons and keep me *firmly* grounded in humility.

I had begun to notice that Chasta was often inside the loafing shed on days when Gaela was grazing contentedly nearby. And her sleeping spot on the ground was a few feet away from the shed and she did not deviate. That in itself seemed odd since she usually had numerous resting places. Was I missing something? She seemed extra quiet and serious, even melancholy. I chalked it up to the fact that she was mirroring my emotions as I responded to my mother's hospitalization and emergency surgery.

My friend Liz Mitten Ryan visited during

this tumultuous time and when Chasta saw us approaching her pasture on the day she was scheduled to leave, called to us with an urgent whinny. She loves Liz, who lives and breathe horses. We both smiled and interpreted her vocalization as recognition that Liz was departing and offering an equine good-bye. When the horses reached us, we scratched their necks and around their ears and then Liz left for her long trip north to the splendor of her sacred *Gateway 2 Ranch* in upper British Columbia, Canada.

Later that evening after visiting with my parents and returning to the pasture by the pond to see the horses, Chasta saw me approaching and thundered toward me calling a shrill whinny. It always thrills me when she really seems happy to see me and this was no exception---in fact, it *especially* made my day after witnessing the difficult physical struggle my Mother was having with no ability on my part to change the situation--- I could only offer support. Gaela was right on Chasta's tail and also seemed especially glad that I was back. *"Hey, girls!"* I called over the fence rails. Chasta continued to nicker with a sense of urgency and used her head to push my arm. She was facing the pond and got behind my back in an attempt to herd me in that direction when I noticed Gaela was running in tight circles like a dog! *Good heavens!* And speaking of dogs, ours started barking wildly and seemed to *really* need my attention, too! What was going on and why was my animal family acting so strange?

Frank, our only remaining duck, heard the commotion and came running from the far end of the pond in response to the sound of my voice for his dinner. Seeing him gave me a sad pang of loss as I promised him again we would find him a female friend. As I headed for his grain bucket, Chasta continued to try and nudge me and I gave her an extra scratch on my way by and tossed Frank a big scoopful of corn. Before he could take his first bite, I heard the loudest rapid fire quacking in the history of duckdom. As I turned in the direction of the unexpected cacophany, from behind a bush at the water's edge emerged Georgia, our female duck, whose feathers were rumpled and sticking out every which way and looking like she hadn't slept in weeks. But she absolutely *sprinted* past me (and you really haven't lived until you have seen a duck truly *run*) grabbed a few lusty bites, and turned and headed back toward the water in the same blazing hurry, corn flying out of her mouth in all directions as she chewed on the fly. Then, rather than scamper down the bank to the pond as ducks do, she took a mighty leaping jump from the edge of the grass bank and landed with a huge belly flop--- *kersplash!*

The horses, dogs, Frank and I all observed the spectacle, our heads turning in unison to watch Georgia's next move. Well, you could have knocked me over with a duck feather! As the wake from her huge splash started to subside, I noticed little black puffy spots surrounding her, bobbing up and down.

My jaw dropped. Oh-my-*gosh*! *Ducklings!!* Real live baby ducks! "Oh, Georgia! You're *alive!!* You *did* it! Frank! Way to go---*great job!*" I hollered out loud. Georgia is a multi-colored duck in khaki tones and Frank is enormous and totally black but for a shimmering green head and his progeny were all complete look-a-likes. I could almost see his cigar as his chest feathers puffed out in pride.

I turned to hug Chasta and in that instant started to put the pieces of the puzzle together. Georgia had tried and failed to nest on her eggs successfully by the edge of the pond even with the comfort and supposed safety of the doghouse. The predators were on to her and the Canadian Geese were like houseguests who stayed too long and get you off your regular rhythms. So Chasta was definitely in on this! "Congratulations, aunties!" I said as I hugged them both and thanked the dogs for their cheerleading. Then I ran like a fool shouting "Oh-my-*gosh!*" repeatedly, tripping over my clogs down the grassy hill to my neighbor Nonie's house.

Working out in her lovely gardens on this perfect summer evening, she overheard my whooping and came around the corner at a good clip, expecting me to be injured and bleeding and found me instead with a big, goofy smile on my face as I proclaimed, "You're a *"Grandmother!"* She looked at me like I had taken leave of my senses as our son had just celebrated his eighteenth birthday and she thought I was referring to him! "We have baby *ducks!*" I hollered foolishly. Now it was her turn to celebrate as she put down her rake and gave me a hearty high five a few weeks before her eighty-first birthday.

We clamored up to the pond and she was as delighted as I was, our first duck brood in domesticity! "Where's the nest?" was her first question. "I'm not sure," I replied, "but it is certain that Chasta was in on it because, as usual, she was *so* aware and trying to tell me." We looked in all of the bushes around the pond without any luck and Nonie suggested that the mother duck often eats the shells of the hatched ducklings for nourishment while she stays on the nest.

When Gary came home that night, we asked him to come down and help us with a project as a decoy to get him to come close enough to the pond to see the surprise, so when he told us he wanted to mow first, I had to spill the beans, and when he saw them for the first time, the look on his face was priceless. "*Baaaa*-by ducks!" he beamed, and rocked back on his heels like a proud Grandpa. With the ridiculously long hours and dedication to his business in a challenging economy this was the most delighted, deep sigh producing smile I had seen in a *long* time. The tired businessman suddenly looked like a young Huck Finn.

The next day Nonie walked up the hill looking like the cat who ate the canary. With a radiant smile from under her wide brimmed sun hat, she posed a question. "I suppose you want to see what *I* found today?!" "*Sure!*" I joined her in the fun, "what is it?" "Just *Georgia's nest* is all!" she teased. "You're kidding! *Where?!*" I begged. With a crooked finger she motioned me to follow and we hiked all the way down the hill to the horses' loafing shed. There on the ground tucked behind a wild elderberry bush on the outside of the shed wall was where Georgia gestated and hatched her family! Good Grief! I turned around and looked at Chasta who was watching me intently. *Now* it all made sense!

I had noticed Chasta staying in the loafing shed on beautiful days when she would normally have been out grazing. I had watched her day after day sleeping on the ground a few feet away from where Georgia was hidden by foliage keeping her eggs warm. As aware as I try to be I had *failed yet again* to connect the dots! This magnificent and maternal horse has apparently convinced a depressed and discouraged little female duck who longed to fulfill her instinctive nature that she was the best bodyguard on the property. Nonie and I looked at the lush and tall green grass that led to the pond and could not conceive of how those tiny little fluff balls made it up the hill to their watery home, but imagine that they were escorted the arduous long distance up the hill by their equine midwife, the amazing Chasta and likely Auntie Gaela, their assistant Nanny. I walked up to Chasta and reminded her that she continues to make my days so filled with joy and wonder that my heart truly overflows with gratitude. And likewise, her personal assistant, the lovely little Pinto pony, Gaela.

Seeing the tender look on my Mother's face, smiling through tears, when I showed her a photo of Frank and Georgia swimming contentedly on their pond with their ducklings as I was telling her the story of Chasta's amazing interspecies communication as she herself was coming to terms with saying goodbye to her own family is another priceless memory I will always remember. Mom and I were both embracing and releasing motherhood as we had known it and had been over the past several years as her need for care increased. She remained my Mother and I her adult child, but the roles were blurring and overlapping. So celebrating maternal joys with the animals nourished us deeply.

And when Evan flew home from a racetrack in Toronto, Canada, to be with his Grandmother following her surgery, seeing the adorable downy feathered new life gave him a respite from the shock and sadness of watching his beloved Grandmother who had always been there for him in his life slip away by degrees.

Later that evening I went down to the pond to say goodnight to all of the animals, checking in on our new water bird family and watching the light from the sunset glow behind the horses in radiant swaths. They approached confidently and in soft tones I told my mares how much they meant to me. I focused on finding their itchy spots and ran my hands down both of their backs, gently scratching with my fingernails. Chasta arched her neck in pleasure as Gaela released a contented snort of exhaled breath.

What happened next has occurred in variations on a theme at other times but this one is forever etched into my heart like the joyful memories of each of us seeing the ducks for the first time are.

With my arms on their backs and fingers gently scratching, Chasta began nibbling quietly on Gaela's withers and in return, Gaela softly touched her muzzle along Chasta's back and down her rump, with fortunate, awestruck, grateful *Me* tightly sandwiched in the middle of those divine animals, sweetly scented soft fur caressing my shoulders. The colors of the sunset surrounding us burst into corals and purples like the finale to a fireworks show and I was melted into the glory of the present moment that morphed into that perfect childhood memory when three horse crazy little girls in a four postered canopied bed fit for a princess shared the reverie of a grooming ritual.

Communication just can not get any better than that.

**Frank and Georgia and their
new ducklings, *at last*!**

Chapter Twenty

Can I Get A Witness?

So much of what I experience with my animals and nature runs the gamut from the ridiculous to the sublime and back again, and when in the midst of these continuously unfolding miracles I often wish there were witnesses. Maybe because they seem so hard to believe and I want my sanity confirmed or to share in the glory of a passion flower bursting into bloom---its layers of chartreuse and purple hues in intricate striped designs like something dreamed up by Dr. Seuss. Or the goofy antics of our dogs when the UPS truck rolls up our long driveway and Cosmo, the Jack Russell terrier clamps his teeth furiously onto the tail of Don, a golden retriever, and is drug in tight running circles as a perfect example of the wonders of centrifugal force. All this while they yip and bark wildly in a burst of canine percussion when seconds earlier they were both sound asleep in the sun in a nearby field. Like dragsters, they can accelerate from zero to zoom in a matter of seconds and become canine whirling dervishes, and then immediately konk out again when the delivery truck rolls out of sight, stopping their activity only long enough to gobble the biscuit our driver has for them.

Or Chasta, on an idyllic summer evening in the lower pasture by the pond looking at me serenely after a long session of having me scratch her itchy spots while she snaked her head down, bobbing it in pleasure and blowing contented snorts into the balmy air, while Gaela grazes peacefully nearby, having already received her massage. Daily I speak to my animals silently as well as with spoken words. When our sessions at liberty came to a natural end in this twilight of August preceding the bursts of pinks and purples of a Western exposure sunset over the farm fields and backdrop of forested islands, Chasta turned to walk away as I heard myself tell her aloud, "You really *are* the queen of the ridge, aren't you? The grand dame of all of the animals here. You care about each of them, but can keep every one in line and make your presence known. You *love* your duck brood but *could* move them, too, any time you wish, I am sure…."

On cue, she advanced in a wide arc toward the unsuspecting ducks who had hunkered down for the evening together nearby, and bent her head down low to the ground with deliberate purpose and summarily popped them, fowl by fowl, into the pond as if they had been pushed in by an invisible leaf blower pointed in their direction. Seeming satisfied, she turned and gave me a look that felt like, "Nice of you to notice and acknowledge my role as matriarch," and walked on. I have never seen her do anything but admire the ducks before or since, and she happily shares the grain that drops when chewing as they crowd her on the ground...

Or the time I was in the round corral with Ritzy, our dear Arabian horse, working on advancing my partnership and abilities as a horsewoman. I had printed the lists of tasks required in the Parelli Natural Horse.Man. Ship™ teaching system off of their website that they term "The Four Savvys." Each area has specific tasks to accomplish on and off line on the ground and on horseback to advance to the next level, establishing an incredible foundation for a lifelong relationship based on trust and understanding. It is a brilliant plan to help humans succeed in learning the nature of the horse and the principles apply in every area of life, but on this day, though my intentions and plan were reasonable enough, I became too interested in the tasks themselves and lost sight of the bigger picture as I put sweet old Ritz though his paces. He was willing and trying his heart out for me, and when each task was achieved satisfactorily, I would take the pen lying next to the stapled sheets of paper atop a large barrel in the center of the corral and triumphantly check it off. (I admit to getting a ridiculous amount of pleasure by checking things off a list, *any* list, and have an enormous desire to create fewer, shorter lists all the time....)

Chasta had been grazing nearby on the other side of the fence when I became aware of her entering the corral through the open gate in my peripheral vision. I turned to acknowledge her when I noticed that she had taken the papers in her teeth and they were dangling like a fan as she glanced over at her best pal, Ritzy, and back at me. "Hey, Chasta," I started calmly, "we need those," as I strode confidently toward her. Her soft eye took on a wild gleam as she spun and took off in the opposite direction and galloped away at top speed, her paper prize fluttering wildly in the breeze created by her thundering circles, enjoying every moment of my dismay. When she had enough of her own pleasure and could see that I chose not to engage by chasing her, the game lost its appeal and she brought them to me like a dog dropping his ball to be thrown. She opened her clenched teeth and released the sodden papers into my hands, while Ritzy and I stood looking at each other, realizing that our session had been long and productive enough. Smiling at both of them, I slipped off his halter and lead rope and promised myself that I would keep those soggy lists as a reminder to be more playful and exuberant (and even a little more *naughty*) like Chasta while I honored my other tendencies to be a willing, hard worker like Ritzy, aiming to please. (And hopefully with fewer, shorter lists…)

And there was the time that Kathy and a number of my horsewomen friends who study natural horsemanship gathered for a playday and Chasta and I enjoyed the game of "property" taught to us by master horseman Jonathan Field for the first time. I had observed it while auditing one of his incredible workshops and was so eager to play! A large space, in this case a fenced pasture, is broken into squares the size of a fifty foot diameter round corral with physical visuals like ground poles and barrels to demarcate the spaces, but allow room for complete movement. Each horse/human pair plays together on the ground on line until harmony is established and then, one horse at a time, the lead ropes come off and the pairs are communicating at liberty. If a horse loses connection and leaves their human and designated area, the *other* humans direct him or her back to their space with driving pressure so that they realize that the place of comfort is with their *own* human. Horses may saunter out of their spaces or bolt, and they are driven back with a matching amount of pressure plus a wee bit more from a distance. This process really helps the horse/human pair bond and the "correction" is by someone else and the reward of comfort is with the horse's own person. It does not take long before the horses understand the game and this allows liberty play to advance quickly and solidly. Periodically, the pairs exchange spaces so that the horses fully understand that the person is the source of comfort, rather than a physical location, such as by the gate.

Chasta understood the game quickly. Sometimes she dashed out and sometimes wandered slowly away, but she knew where the boundary lines were because she put a hoof over the line in every direction to test the waters. When she did that, my watchful friends would swing a rope in her direction, aimed at the body part that needed to move back to me.

Finally she decided life was best sticking close to me and we hooked up and walked together, then rested and lingered in the center to allow her to soak it in while I petted her quietly. Then I asked, apparently for the moon, when I sent her out at the trot on a circle to the left, something she did with total ease at that time in the round corral, but this space was wide open by comparison.

I watched in amazement as this remarkable mare trotted in circles within the perimeter of our square, yet attempting to lean outside the circle. She was bent beautifully to the left and her feet were moving on their diagonals in a rhythmic way. I stood watching her, riveted to how much she could comply while not complying! Her position did not even look physically *possible* or comfortable in any way. Her eye looked totally soft and calm, as did the rest of her body language. Chasta seems to like to do things *her* way, and usually tries. The amount of physical effort she was expending to make her point was *huge*. I asked her to the center, gave her praise for what she *did* do well, and suggested she go out on a circle in the other direction which she did willingly with another good bend in her body and her head *inside* the circle, but seemingly folded at the ankle joints attempting to lean outside the boundary! She not only defied me, but the laws of physics! Skilled horsepeople that I know feel that Chasta will *always* be asking me, *"Are you my leader?"* Often, I am able to tell her assuredly, *"Yes, I am!"* And the rest of the time, I remain rigorously honest when I tell her, *"Lord knows that I am trying to be!"*

Observing Chasta's behavior often leaves me asking more questions than I have answers for. I could see the value of this game and realized that if played properly by the humans, it could have very positive effects. Horses understand being driven out of another horse's territory---it is a part of their internally coded language system. And the secondary benefit is that when the other participants push an invading horse away and guard their own, it is viewed by their horse as protective and garners respect while increasing their bond.

So while in theory it seems like a good practice, I find myself constantly questioning what is the best decision for Chasta. She is no doubt a horse who wants choices. Any level of coercion can ignite something in her that creates brace and defensiveness. When Alex Hailey's epic book series, *Roots*, first appeared on television, Gary and I watched with great interest and heartache. Later we viewed it again with our son,

Evan, when it aired for the 25th anniversary of its debut, grateful that we could discuss the trials and triumphs of the story as a family. It was shortly after Chasta had entered my life and I was struck with the parallels between her and the character of Kunta Kinte. So many of the captured African people were beaten into submission, their spirits broken, so they became obedient and submissive based on fear. And yet there were individuals who chose to fight or run, which are also the natural responses of a horse to fear. Horses have been similarly forced to do the bidding of man and the number who are willing to go into fight or flight are often labeled as difficult, defective or dangerous.

So when Chasta shows me a lack of acceptance to my suggestion, I *must* ask myself: Does she understand what I am asking? Is it necessary? Is it fun? Is it fair? Is it interesting? Is it safe? Is she physically able to do it? Am I? Is it in our best interest as partners? Chasta is not my possession, nor am I hers. We are friends, companions. United souls. Teacher and student. Student and teacher. Hopefully she knows how much I am listening to hear *her* questions, and enencouraging her to ask them.

Often I *do* have other humans to witness my

experiences and the gifts given by the natural world all around us with their own two eyes, appreciative ears and tender hearts. My son Evan is the first one to spot a spectacular sunset or a soaring eagle and bring it to our attention, often saying a quiet *"Amen"* to himself in recognition. And my husband Gary talks to the animals as much as I do. He is obviously their kindred spirit and benevolent sponsor.

My dear friend Kathy Yaeger, who has been my greatest teacher in advancing my skills with horses, trims my mares' hooves regularly so that they can go barefoot naturally. Thanks to Joe Camp telling his wonderful story from the horses' point of view in his bestselling book, *The Soul of a Horse*, more horses are now barefoot the way Nature intended them to be. One day during a trim, Kathy asked Chasta to stretch her left front hoof forward onto the stand so that she could create the final rolled edge with a file. With a huge sigh and *very* little effort, Chasta grudgingly obliged as if it were asking the *world*. Undaunted, Kathy said "Oh, *goodness,* Chasta---you can do better than *that!* This is *hardly* a stretch for a big, strong, smart ballerina like *you!*" I smiled, loving to hear Kathy spar with this marvelously intelligent horse in her delightful British accent that reveals her roots. Finishing the hoof, she thanked Chasta in a tone of mock appreciation, saying that she knew it was *really* a challenge and told her that she could now take it off the stand and put it down.

Chasta no sooner had that hoof on the mat when she looked with care at both of us to see that we were paying attention and took her left *hind* leg and stretched it up with complete ease to scratch long and lavishly between her ears! If words had accompanied her gesture, they likely would have been: "You ladies want a *stretch?! This* is what I can do whenever I *choose!*" When she was sure that her message had been received, she casually put her foot down quietly and Kathy finished the job in perfect harmony, chuckling with appreciation for the perspective offered to us by these amazing animal companions that we are so blessed to know.

So though I *do* have many credible, certifiably sane humans as my witnesses to what I have experienced over the years, ultimately all that matters is what I perceive through the lens from which I see, the awareness that I hear, and the huge range of sensations that I feel. It is really between God and Me.

You may think that I might become an eccentric old woman with sixteen cats, a pack of silly dogs, wandering the property in a tattered robe and fuzzy slippers, scratching the horses and feeding the ducks, with lipstick on my teeth. And that is a distinct possibility since the wheels are already in motion. But the glory of God is all around me and I cannot help but notice and offer thanks and praise.

Can I get a witness?

Passion Flower

Photo by Dr. Michael Bart

Chapter Twenty One

Defining Moments

In the early evening of the day my mother died, I sat down with my sister and niece to write the obituary with Mom's stilled body lying across the room in the home that our father/grandfather designed. The task of capturing the essence that was our mother/grandmother was enormous and daunting. How could we possibly express all the moments that defined her life as daughter, friend, granddaughter, wife, mother, grandmother, volunteer, school secretary, child of God?

Yet I felt incredibly blessed that she died at home with people who knew and loved her deeply. And that the funeral director was our neighbor and friend and had been holding all of us in her personal prayers. When the director arrived, she warmly embraced my family and somehow maintained her professional dignity while consoling us and facing the personal loss of a woman who had supported her own children significantly in the small town where we are blessed to call home. While my sisters and niece comforted our father/grandfather as he faced the mind and body numbing shock of the death of his life partner of fifty-six years, I sat with the director to complete the necessary paperwork.

She filled in the information that I gave her and my behavior and composure was that of an emotionally agile adult until she gave me a form that my mother had filled out years before she was ever ill. It expressed her desires for a memorial service that matched what our family had painfully attempted to discuss with her shortly before her death. Seeing her familiar *Kay-Mom-Grandma* at the bottom of the form, the way she had always signed cards and greeted us on the telephone, and a personal message in her own handwriting caused me to weep as a small child, wanting her mother.

While the director waited for me to regain my composure, she turned the paperwork toward me again and asked for my signature and I realized that the baton had been passed. I could feel my hand shake reaching for the pen and recalled the moment that my mother held her newborn grandson, Evan, in the waiting room of our physician's office on the morning of his first check-up. I was filling out the new patient form and as I did, turned the paper to show her the very first time that I had penned his complete name since his birth. She beamed at me without words and it was one of the most special moments that we ever shared. I continued entering the information when at the bottom of the page there was a line that read: *Relationship to patient* followed by a blank space. For some reason, I felt temporarily stumped until it hit me. I was Evan's *mother*. Surely that came as no surprise, yet I had never recorded it. Looking up, I saw Mom cooing at Evan and when she caught my eye, I put my finger on the line that said *Mother*, followed by my signature and this time our smiles created tears of connection in this defining, tender moment.

Thirty four years earlier, my mother had signed *her* name as a much younger mother on *my* new patient paperwork. Coming full circle, now it was my turn to add mine at fifty three to the bottom of her death certificate as daughter. Tears flowed again as I felt the comfort of my neighbor's hands on mine and within a few more minutes, my mother's physical form was rolled out the door and left my life. Only her ashes would remain to bury and scatter and the memories of who she was to each of us. Holding the maternal baton, I realized that I would run with it in my own strength by the grace of God and make deliberate choices and that my journey has been far different than hers and also very similar. As I move forward, my desire is to honor my mother and *continue to hear my own true voice, my connection to the inner divinity* that is our gift. I must learn daily to balance nurturing myself and serving and supporting others.

My husband Gary and son Evan have provided me with incredible support through these difficult yet grace filled times and I will always feel gratitude for the fact that Evan was able to return home to thank his grandmother, a final time, for the love that she offered him throughout his life.

A few months later it was time for Evan and I to fly east to pack his belongings and drive back home to his roots where he had chosen to return to rewrite and pursue his dreams with a completely new level of gratitude and life awareness. We loaded a truck and trailer and over the next few days, said goodbye to his first experience away from home, laughing and crying together over the memories. We carefully packed the painting of a Northwest farm scene that was created by his grandfather Glen that was his Grandmother Kay's personal favorite. She had *insisted* that her grandson take it when he moved east, knowing that he liked it the most as well. And my father's Medal of Honor from the US Navy that had been on Evan's fireplace mantle next to a small container of ashes from his beloved childhood companion, a sixteen year old black lab named Hooter, who had died two days before he left to make the cross country trek. That trip was made driving with Evan's other grandparents---his paternal Grandmother JoAnn and his grandfather by marriage, Robert, who had sung together to the music on the radio the entire time, creating a lifetime bond. When Evan packed and left for his first race on the road, they were there to send him off with love and support.

We wrapped a blanket around an enlarged vintage photograph of Evan's biological paternal grandfather, Charlie, who had died before he was born, winning a race in his old jalopy on a dirt track that was the start of a three generation love of racing between father, son and grandson. I was also especially careful to wrap the photos of Evan's girlfriend, Devyn, and her horse Dan, and the ones of the happy faced teenagers together at the homecoming dance.

Memories flooded me as I remembered my brother's beautiful and heartfelt tenor voice sing *Danny Boy* while he played his guitar at our Mother's memorial service as he had for

Devyn and her Danny Boy

her over the years since it was her favorite song from childhood that her own father had sung to her. And sweet Devyn, when she got the call from Evan that his grandmother had passed on, just as she was about to go out to perform in competition with the horse she affectionately calls *Danny Boy.* Through her tears, she composed herself and asked Dan to give them the ride of their lives. He knew his purpose and they won Grand Champions together and earned a berth to the state event.

Feeling tears saturate my eyes, I closed them and could picture the tall, dark, angular features of Father Patrick Twohy, a priest who lovingly served the Swinomish and Tulalip tribal communities for over twenty years. Knowing him originally from a distance, one time after stretching together at a local Yoga class, I asked him what his tribal heritage was, since I had assumed that he was a Native American. "My tribe?" he smiled. "I am a Jesuit—and Black Irish." His eyes twinkled when I seemed surprised. At a celebration honoring him when he left to serve the urban Native American population of Seattle, he was the quiet and humble giant of a man who we had become accustomed to seeing in jeans and handmade wool native Cowichian sweaters. As each elder rose to speak in thanks and praise, Father Pat kept his head low, a sincere smile on his face and raised his arms in tribute to the people that he loved so dearly. Finally, a beautiful young man from the Tulalip tribe rose to address his friend and mentor. "Father Pat cares deeply for all of us and respects and honors our ways. He has learned our language, our dances, our drumming. *He is one of us.* So today, I honor him with a song from *his* homeland." He proceeded to sing every verse of *Danny Boy,* acappella, as tenderly as my brother had for my Mother. Father Twohy has been able to share his own faith traditions because he honored those of the people he served. He wrote a beautiful book about the Coast Salish Peoples reclaiming their culture called *Beginnings* with some of his own poetry and interviews with tribal members that show the essence of the beauty of his relationship with them. Every American should watch a documentary film called *Our Spirits Don't Speak English* about the Indian Boarding School era where Indians were stripped of their language and traditions and coerced to adopt the ways of the Euro-Anglo government and churches. The irony that this country was founded on religious and cultural freedom and then turned around and took it away from others who preceded their arrival has contributed to multi-generational suffering that we must continue to address as a nation in order to heal. Father Patrick Twohy is a model for the love in action that crosses all traditions.

As Evan and I continued to pack boxes, we enjoyed a steady stream of trick-or-treaters in this quiet suburban neighborhood in Indiana and felt grateful that we could reciprocate for the famous "Hoosier Hospitality" that we had received during the time we set Evan up in housekeeping there. Though he only returned to the house infrequently during his race season on the road, he felt a sense of the kindness of community there that sustained him.

The first day we headed toward home, our goal was to get close to Evan's midwest based Godfamily. We enjoyed un-seasonally warm weather and an outdoor fire with friends who had become family over the years and loved savoring a home cooked meal and warm beds and most of all to meet their first grandchild---the son of his oldest Godsister and her husband who was passed around to each of us and adored by all. I remembered sharing a precious birth photo of him with my mother seven months earlier, reassuring us that life truly goes on. Since the state zoo was in their neighborhood and the November weather was in the 70s, we took a nice break and enjoyed being outside and seeing the wonders of the world we live in. Both Evan and I so wished that his cousin's son Rylan, nearly three, could have been there with us. Focusing on the importance of family, youth and new beginnings was such was a comfort.

We took a loop off of the interstate to stop at the sacred burial grounds of the battlefields of Little Bighorn. Tragic as the circumstances, it is American history and I felt compelled to plant my feet firmly on the earth in that beautiful place and offer my arms to the heavens in memory and honor of each soul who died there. It hurt my heart to think that these bloody battlefields still rage around the world and I prayed for the peace *that I know is possible* as we learn to truly love and forgive ourselves and others as we *strive for a balanced model of lead mare and stallion, yin and yang, Mother Earth and Father Sky as a world culture.* We *must* shift our thinking to a level of wholism and cooperation if our planet is to survive. Evan and I were heartened by the local Native Americans with their Anglo neighbors working side by side in harmony as we were paying our respects.

One of the most heart wrenching moments for us came as we stood not only amidst the graves of the fallen US Army soldiers and Indians, but also their equine partners, the calvary mounts and native ponies. Cathartic sobs cleansed me as I rooted myself to the ground near their buried bones, knowing they were pressed into service by both sides of the dispute. The panoramic view of mountains surrounding us were filled with dots in the distance of the grazing horses of today and though they no longer carry humans to war, *thank God,* their purpose is still determined by man and they continue to offer the nobility of partnership that defined the tragic history recorded there.

Evan and I enjoyed a delicious lunch at the Native Trading Post and purchased gifts to share. Grateful for their hospitality, I was reminded of the beautiful customs of our local Swinomish Tribal Community at home and the unparalleled warmth and generosity of their spirits and how much mine has been nourished whenever we have attended one of their celebrations over the years. And I felt so thankful to reflect how closely our local school district works in partnership with the tribe to improve what is offered educationally so that the native students can learn their nearly forgotten language and reclaim the customs that made their culture so strong. To truly understand the teachings of their ancestors before they were assimilated into the white culture by our government.

Bronze Sculpture behind the Sacred Circle burial ground at Little Bighorn

I applaud the efforts of people like Percy White Plume, a Lakota Native, who organizes a 350 mile horseback ride for students from South Dakota to the site of the massacre of Wounded Knee on its anniversary each December. The planning and experience of this trip becomes living history and is a truly transformational journey for the children to reclaim their heritage as strong and proud people of the horse. After surviving this arduous trip, and seeing all the people along the way who support them, they learn to make good choices and are able to heal some of the generational woundedness that has afflicted our nation. We can look for ways to support the many groups like the one that Percy has created to be a part of this healing and growth process. You can learn more about Percy and many others by logging onto my friend Robin Carneen's radio station: NAMAPAHH, which stands for Native American Multi-Media, Activism, Performance/poetry, Art, Health/Humor/History.

US Calvary Horse cemetery

Hours later, my son and I high-fived as we crossed the Continental Divide, coming through snow flurries and a wild hail storm and then were welcomed into the valley of the town of Butte, Montana, by a marble sculpture called *Our Lady of the Rockies,* an enormous non-denominational white maternal silhouette tucked into the mountainside and backlit by the moon and manmade lights.

After a local meal, we settled into our hotel room beds for the second leg of our American history-making day just in time for the final commentary before the projected election returns on CNN announced the new presidency of Barack Obama. Evan and I were truly impressed by the extraordinarily gracious and heartfelt concession speech by John McCain, after such a divisive campaign, which we felt set the positive tone for the evening and then waited expectantly for the appearance of the elected candidates and their families and supporters.

Anyone in my age group and older can likely remember where they were when President John F. Kennedy was elected, and tragically, as I mention in the foreword to this book, his assassination and funeral. In all of my years as a voter, I have never felt a similar emotionally charged, hope filled and bittersweet defining moment as I did since those days of my early childhood when the nation desperately needed to unite with each other after a contentious election. The eloquence of Mr. Obama as he shared the story of Ann Nixon Cooper, the 106 year old black woman who had lived through all of the historic defining moments and was able to be counted in voting for the first African American president of the United States touched me so deeply as I again prayed for each person of every race, creed, color, religion, age and gender on that history making night.

It struck me that people are very much like horses in that as different as we are, *we are all very much the same*. While we were at the zoo in Minnesota, though we love barnyard animals and would have enjoyed seeing their display of domestic horses, since those are familiar to us, we focused on the wild animals in the time frame we felt we had. As we were leaving the exhibits and heading toward the parking lot after seeing the Bengal tigers and other exotics, we came upon something that I had only hoped to see in my lifetime---the true wild horses of Asia! Known as Equus przwatskii, they are considered the only pure remaining herds of wild horses in the world today who have not intermingled with some domestic horses, and were nearly extinct in the steppes of outer Mongolia and it turns out this zoo had been instrumental in being able to acquire and breed some in captivity and then in cooperation with the Chinese Government, reintroduce them to their original environment to increase natural herd populations. I saw the sign and felt a tingle shoot up my spine in hopes of actually seeing them and then on this amazing warm November day in a month where there is often deep snow, a small herd came down the hill as if on cue to present themselves, two weanlings among them! I thanked God for continuing to show me that life is *so* incredibly rich and beautiful and that I *must focus* on what is good and right and share that love and wonder with everyone I encounter. These horses looked very much like the domestic Norwegian Fjord horse that belongs to our good friends Joanne and Mike. And yet they looked significantly different from my friend Marylin's mini horses, and my master horseman friend, Jonathan Field's black Andalusian stallion. *But not really.*

What I mean by this is that *all* horses, regardless of color, size, gender and age, are *so* much more similar than different, regardless of whether they are wild or domestic or where they live or what breed they are. Their anatomy and physiology is that of the species Equus and so is their behavior and their need for survival. They are mammals like us and have emotions and express love and dependence upon their family systems and have an enormous need for community. They share territory and were designed for their respective environments. The fact that the Equus przwatskii is the final remaining wild horse attests to the reality that breeds all over the world have co-mingled and actually, many of the cross breeds have acquired a hybrid vigor that gives them the best of all of their ancestry. As we watched people of all races and colors celebrate the success of their candidate, I could not help but feel that people all over the world have done the same thing. In fact, Mr. Obama himself is of multi racial origins.

It fascinates me that I was given the sacred gift of Chasta six years ago the year I was forty seven, and Barack Obama the same age as he accepted the role of leader of this great nation. Naturally, there is an *absolutely enormous* contrast between the level of our roles and at the same time, very little difference in the actual playing out of our efforts. I am learning through my natural horsemanship and equine guided development studies to become the very *best individual* that I can be. A leader in my own life, in my partnership with Chasta and Gaela, family and community. Each of us is called to action and must take responsibility to heed the call. Growing and learning with my mares has helped me to find my voice and to become a spokesperson for those who need support for theirs to be heard---the horses, the trees, the children, the oceans.....

In an earlier chapter, I cite the collective *pain-body* of the American consciousness described by Eckhart Tolle in his book, *The New Earth*, and how much we all need to forgive and heal, particularly for the injustices done to African Americans, women, the Native American Indians, other minorities, animals, children and the environment.

I have a profound memory of a defining moment of perhaps the first time my concept of pain as an important messenger to healing was realized. During the years of active alcoholism in our marriage, I was at the peak of my unhealthy adaptive codependent behaviors and joined a guided recovery group for women. The counselor who led us started the initial meeting giving us an overview of what the sessions would cover and asked that we go around the circle and introduce ourselves and share some background information. When it was my turn, I launched into what *appeared* to be a confident dissertation of how I had researched the disease and was well versed in the recovery process and that I knew exactly what my husband needed to do and...blah, blah, blah.... In mid-sentence, I was abruptly cut off by the leader who said bluntly: "Connie, we can see that you are plenty smart, but being smart is *not* what brought you here. You came here because you were in enough *pain*." And then she motioned for the next person to share. *Ouch!* There I sat, mute and red-faced while some of the women looked at me with compassion and others turned their heads to focus awkwardly at their feet, likely happy that my speech had been quickly ended. I could feel my gut tighten with the impact of the emotional blow to my solar plexus that this truth had triggered. As much as I was taken aback in that moment, it was the beginning of my recognition of pain on every level as a life saving messenger and to allow it to cut through the numbness of suppression and denial. Pain today in every form is my friend (though sometimes I still do not see it as such) since it always has information for me to respond to. It is a symptom of some deeper truth that I need to feel. If I mask it by ignoring or killing the messenger with a drug, a material purchase or even "busyness" it will come again to visit, often more harshly than before. The fact that the counselor chose to cut to the chase and tell me the truth was one of my greatest gifts and life lessons I have ever received. It allowed me to truly hear, see and feel. It was a profound beginning.

This election success will continue to do much to heal those old wounds and we must work together as a nation to insure that they do not reopen, but rather to form beautiful scars that we can continue to learn from and be inspired by. What amazing opportunities we all have to heal and grow---such an exciting time in history to be alive! I do not fully agree with every decision made by Mr. Obama, but there are not two people who agree on everything anywhere. We must learn to live in a world where we can sometimes agree to disagree with respect and in harmony. My heart is hopeful for tremendous long-term positive change.

Hopeful in the way I felt reading Brian McLaren's landmark book, *Everything Must Change: Jesus, Global Crises, and a Revolution of Hope.* Brian McLaren asks the all important question: How do the life and teachings of Jesus address the most critical global problems of our world today? He candidly addresses what he calls our "suicidal social, economic and political dysfunctional systems" and invites us to examine the core message of faith teachings to lead us to peace, abundance and environmental sustainability in a global community. He sees a bigger, richer picture and is a leader who thinks like a contemporary Saint Francis. His writing and thoughtful suggestions infuse me with enthusiasm. Like Barack Obama, he is igniting a revolution of hope that *can* change everything that requires change. Both men agree that it needs to start with each of us. *Now.* And the most beautiful thought in all of these extreme challenges and necessary and difficult changes that we face is that the only thing that will *never* change is God's unfailing love for us. *All* of us.

During our road trip on that historic day, Evan and I listened to a CD series, also in book form, called *Spontaneous Evolution*, presented by Dr. Bruce Lipton, famous for his incredible work described in his first book, *The Biology of Belief*, and Steve Bhaerman, aka Swami Beyondananda, the Cosmic Comic. These remarkable men are very well educated and intuitive pioneers, leading the way to a healthier, more wholistic future for all of us. Using both sides of their brains, they lead by the information from the knowledge gained in scholarly research and guided by their inner spiritual knowings, insuring a balance between science and the divine. Not one or the other, but both. The information presented gave Evan and I incredible opportunities for dialogue about some of the dysfunction in our family systems, starting with ourselves and our immediate families and projecting outward. We realized fully that we are a microcosm of the macrocosm and felt truly grateful for the level of healing and understanding that we have experienced thus far. These discussions were on a level that I so longed for with my own parents at that age and we vowed to continue them and keep the lines of communication open.

As Mahatme Ghandi stated so brilliantly:

"We must be the change that we seek."

Faith. Hope. Love.

One still, small voice at a time.

My Mother

Kathleen Janet Peck Bartlett
February 16, 1936-August 7, 2008

Kay with Babe and Kitty

"Death is not the opposite of life~
Life has no opposite
The opposite of death is birth~
Life is eternal"

Eckhart Tolle

Chapter Twenty Two

Much Ado About Poop

When did the natural bodily functions of life become so unnatural and uncomfortable for us as a culture? For example: Waste production. Certainly we inherited some of the Puritanical views of our ancestors directly and some from the collective consciousness as interpreted by Madison Avenue, trying to keep us powdered and odor free. Now healthy modesty is one thing, and guilty shame is quite another.

I remember my dear maternal grandmother who my family affectionately called "Nanny" asking me as a small child if I had to go "wee-wee" or "big toe toe." It was a bit puzzling for me since we had completely different terms at home and then the issue was further confused when I entered Kindergarten and my teacher called it "Number 1 and Number 2."

The s-word was definitely taboo in my home

unless you actually hit your thumb accidentally with a hammer, and though the word "crap" was one that sometimes snuck into my Mother's vocabulary in unexpected moments, "poop" became the least objectionable term. Not exactly warm and fuzzy, but tolerable. I remember Evan using the word crap in frustration as a toddler, so I gently reminded him that when Winnie the Pooh and Piglet felt discouraged, they used terms like: *"Oh, Bother!"* and *"Bumblebees"* or *"Fiddlesticks!"* He looked up at me resolutely and replied *"Grandma says it!"* He had a point.

And of his many fond memories from childhood, a favorite was the time when he spent the evening with his grandparents eating homemade brownies that he and Grandma concocted and enjoying his own can of pop (something that his organic whole foods oriented Mother would not have provided) while the three of them got into a rousing game of Monopoly™. As the game progressed, Grandpa acquired Park Place and Boardwalk, the most elite properties, and mortgaged them to purchase hotels. Shrewd move. Grandma rolled the dice and came around and landed smack dab on Boardwalk, causing her immediate financial ruin, and before she could think, hollered *"Shit!"* and then spent the rest of the evening blushing, giggling girlishly and apologizing to her grandson who was equally delighted and shocked. I mean, it was his *Grandmother!*

I spend a good portion of my time scooping poop on the small acreage where we live. We have always enjoyed a collection of dogs, and horses are especially voluminous producers. It is easy to appreciate the tidy habits of cats who carefully bury their solid waste discretely----such noble creatures! I admit to not relishing chicken and dog waste which I regularly toss over the fence back into our burn pile area so that we don't step into it and I am careful in the garden and around the pond not to slip in duck poo, with it's slippery consistency that nourishes the soil.

But horse poop is just not that objectionable---they eat grass, and it helps my compost piles break down faster and become richer. And besides, it is all just merely a by-product of energy production, that which animates our lives. If my marvelous horses create liquid and solid waste easily and regularly, it means they are healthy—and that is a *good* thing.

And the more I hang out with horses and scoop and schlep their poop, the more I relax about my *own* releases being anything but

302

ordinary and natural and when focused on being truly grateful for the grand design of creation, and my small but significant part in it, *miraculous*.

Though horses' bowels can certainly be affected by emotional feelings such as fear which can cause quick and loose evacuation, most of the time, it is accomplished without any fanfare whatsoever. Just business as usual. Natural as can be. Just stop, drop and move on, back to grazing. Right there in front of God and everyone.

And it still surprises me to recall and wonder why I felt the urge to recoil in disgust in my college years when my talented artist brother created a cartoon for the campus newspaper about the fact that people needed to know where their poop goes. As in take responsibility for it. And he was right. We *should* know and care about our own personal waste and that which we create in our environment, and it should not be someone else's problem. We need to be aware of the bigger picture and our role to keep the planet as healthy as possible. But at that time it seemed so crude to me — so *personal*.

But birds do it. Bees do it. Even educated fleas do it. In this case, not fall in love like the old standards goes, but *create waste*. I guess we all just need to lighten up (no pun intended here), but we would do well to lose the shame and embarrassment that often comes with it.

With children, it is a totally natural process and we expect to change diapers until such time that a choice can be made to use a toilet. And if that process is supported in a healthy manner (I remember we had paper targets that floated in the toilet bowl that gave Evan wonderful incentive to stand on a stool and take careful aim...) it goes a long way to help a child feel confident and relaxed and in touch with their beautiful bodies. And we all know of the consequences of shame in that department.

My father's very first memory was of his angry and impatient Mother taking a small redheaded neighbor girl in her care by the hair and rubbing her nose on the floor in the urine she created by accident while scolding her harshly like a puppy, completely unjust behavior that creates total fear and confusion in children and animals. It is a horrifying thought and has disturbed my Father deeply his entire life. He was so frightened by his Mother's lack of tenderness and the powerlessness that he felt for himself and the little girl for something that he knew on some level as a small boy was completely natural.

So if in a healthy outlook these regular movements of the bowels and emptying of the bladder is a normal, expected process in children, why do we find it so repugnant in adults when due to aging or illness that incontinence becomes an issue? I don't have a good answer for that because as loving and calm as I always tried to be for my Mother when it became a challenge for her, it was admittedly difficult for me to help her adjust to our role reversal and help her accept that she needed to wear a diaper, much less have me change it. Why is that? As a mother, I did not think twice about it for my own son, no matter the contents. Truthfully, it was not my most favorite task, but I did it without impatience, discomfort, judgment or anxiety. It was purely *developmental.* And it was my role—my gift as a mother.

But for a woman who is in a physical decline and can no longer feel in control of those functions, it can wreak havoc with her emotions, and those of her adult child. My sweet Mother would apologize profusely as we would freshen her up in the bathroom after an accident and I would launch into my usual schpiel that went something like: "Mom?! Did you ever change my diapers?!" Pause. *"Mom?"* "Yes, I did," she would quietly reply, head down. "And did you get any help?" I would press further. Pause. "Well, no." was her response. And since I have a sister fifteen months older and a brother thirteen months younger, it means that conceivably that there was a period when she was single handedly changing diapers for three children X number of times per day, week and year! I figured out that she was likely at least a thousand diapers ahead of me and owed her big time, but that did little to relieve either of us of some of the discomfort.

Oh, we had some comic relief. Regularly agreeing that the situation was the pits between gales of laughter. *No question!* There were many public restrooms that in no way had space for two women, their purses and a walker inside the stall but we managed to wiggle into them to get the job done. My sister sent me a great cartoon with an old gal in a flowered hat pushing her walker forward with a determined look and a sign attached, "Washroom or Bust." We couldn't decide whether Mom would laugh or if it would just make her feel badly, so I erred on the side of caution and put it up on my bulletin board at home so I could help maintain my perspective and not feel so alone in my challenge and keep my own humor intact, so as to best help my Mother.

After an operation to repair my Mother's bowels, her surgeon asked if she had passed gas following the anesthesia as she recovered. When she hesitated to respond, he smiled kindly and said, "Not just a little, it has to be long and loud enough to make a fifth grader laugh!" My mother blushed, but smiled broadly with a tiny giggle and said quietly, "Not yet!" So I asked him if his children had grown up with a book that Mom had gifted Evan with when he was a small fellow called: *The Gas We Pass: The Story of Farts.* Now it was his turn to chuckle and we had a relaxed conversation about this universal bodily function. The book, written for children of all ages by Shinto Cho is filled with facts and humor and delightful illustrations and was a favorite read for Mom and her grandson. No matter how many times the two of them enjoyed it together, they always laughed hysterically, a great memory for me, shaking my head in amusement from the other room.

So why have I rambled on so long about fecal matter? Excrement? Urination? Because it *happens!* Like death and taxes, it is inevitable for all of us. Into every life a little poop must fall. Not to mention number 1. And I promise you that my Mother would not cringe for me to share this experience, because, like me, she agreed that *if it helps even one elder parent/adult child pair have an easier time finding the humor and grace, all while attempting to maintain dignity without shame in this situation,* then she was absolutely in favor of it. She graced me with her permission.

After all, these can be the ties that bind. Or loosen, as the case may be. So let's focus on the fact that we are all in this physical form with our always glorious if less than perfectly functional bodies together.

And while we are at it, please gentlemen, *kindly remember to put the seat down.*

Evan and Chad produce black gold compost together

Chapter Twenty Three

Transitions

Horses make transitions look easy. In equine vernacular, transitions are the ease of movement between one gait and another. Upward transitions are marked by increasing speed and downward by slowing the pace. Natural athletes, horses inherently know the ballet of fluid movement from birth. Since equines are a precocial species, they have this capacity from their beginning. In the wild, the ability of a foal to start moving with the herd shortly after hitting the ground may dictate survival. Within hours, this new creature will mimic the movement of his or her mother by resting, walking, trotting and finding the easy cadence of a soft loping run. Horses are born to run, and surely describe how the "hit the ground running expression" originated.

The natural modus operendi of the species Equus is movement. Forever foraging for what sustains them, their hardwired instincts lead them to vegetation and water, always putting one foot in front of the other. Observing either wild or domestic horses, watching their ease of movement from a standstill to an all out gallop and back again can be astonishing and may easily take your breath away. Truly poetry in motion.

Adding a rider can change that natural snapshot completely. Once a horse is well trained to accommodate a rider, most will tolerate the learning curve of the human to find natural balance in each gait by maintaining their center of gravity with the movement and weight shifts of the horse.

That was certainly the case with our first horse, Chad. After a lifetime of loving and aching for horses and not having one of my own, we acquired acreage, fenced it and built a stable. Since I was forty and my son was five, we took the advice of horse people we talked with and looked for a quiet, well-trained older horse. This is where the grace of God comes in because that is exactly who Chad was.

Chad had been there and done that. He started life as a ranch horse and had been owned and loved after his beginnings by three unrelated young girls who took him through every conceivable discipline with each possible configuration of tack and living situation. He was a thoughtful and willing horse in mind, body and spirit and always aimed to please. When people questioned why we did not get a pony for our small child instead of a barrel chested Quarter horse, one look at the soulful brown eyes of this lovely old sorrel chestnut and his gentle ways dispelled any doubt.

Because Chad was so patient with me learning to ride a horse at midlife, I started to understand how to lean slightly forward at the walk where the highest percentage of the horse's weight is on their forehand, then back to center at the trot when it is fifty –fifty, and when I kissed him up to the three beated canter with some uncertainty, he ran in slow motion like a rocking horse to help me stay steady. If I was out of balance going into a turn, Chad would come up under me to compensate. Slowly, patiently, he helped me to gain confidence and become a fairly well balanced passenger, riding with only a lead rope and halter tied off. I only had to *think* faster or slower and he would accommodate me.

I knew that Chad was a special horse. A gentle giant. He was grateful for his quiet retirement where his duties were light and his pastures were green. But when he died, I was left not only broken hearted, but also very naïve. My limited world view of horses was through the lens of Chad. He was willing to partner with me regardless of my requests because he understood my need---my heart and desire for him---and was willing to fill in to meet me in the middle. What I did not fully realize until he was gone was that Chad was *extraordinary. Exceptional.* No question the ideal first horse. For *anyone.*

Enter Chasta. If Chad's overall demeanor was willing, hers was wary. Everything that had been easy for me with Chad was difficult with Chasta. Whatever confidence I had developed learning with Chad did not seem to transfer to her. She exposed me to my underlying fears and uncertainty and did *not* want an unfocused, unbalanced rider on her back. My fear and frustration revealed anger and feelings of rejection and abandonment beneath the surface and caused me to have to take a good hard look at how ill-equipped in my mind, body, spirit and emotions I was to be her competent partner.

It was time for me to become the driver of my destiny rather that a passenger on the ship of life. Chasta arrived nearly a decade after Chad to help me co-pilot my way to the heavenly realms on earth, but with this mare, I had to *earn* my wings.

When I am horseback with Chasta, she requires that I *pay attention*. Have *a plan*. Be *fully* engaged and integrated in mind, body and spirit, *not merely coming along for the ride*. She has taught me to completely *feel* my emotions, and to be present in the moment with each as I move through the day with a much greater level of awareness and gratitude for life.

I took Chad for granted. Completely. He allowed me to be on cruise control. Not so with Chasta. She snapped me out of auto-pilot and *insisted* that I take the wheel. She brought me up close and personal with my utter reliance and need for God and at the same time introduced me to my own personal power, liberally dosed with down on my knees humility.

My life lessons learning to maintain my balance on every level horseback has been providing me with a roadmap for moving through transitions as a wife, mother, daughter and friend. Chasta lifted my veil. And not always so gently. But she knew it was time. And necessary. Even *urgent*.

I was no longer the mother of a small child

playing in the sand with trucks. As I was preparing Thanksgiving dinner the year Evan was in middle school, he leaned over the kitchen counter and asked me thoughtfully, "*Mom*, could I ask you a question?" "Sure," I answered, wondering about his serious tone. "Could we redecorate my bedroom?" Surprised, I replied with, "Of course, but what brought that up?" Evan was racing and beating adults in his sprint car on a regular basis at this time in his life and patiently, he took a deep breath to give me an answer, looking at me sweetly and attempting to be delicate. "I'm almost fourteen and there are still toddler sized antique sailor suits hanging from my pegracks!" It's not like he wasn't reminded of them enough since there are huge portraits of him wearing them, looking like Buster Brown, throughout our home. I was living in a time warp.

And who was that silver haired woman in the mirror? It wasn't my mother yet I looked just like her. Recently I used a washcloth to attempt to wipe off what I thought was a pen mark on my face until I realized it was a line that was etched in! *Yikes!*

It felt like yesterday that I was redecorating *my* bedroom when I was in junior high school, painting the walls and ceiling in huge flowers like in a tropical jungle. Then in no time it seemed that I left home for college, got married, worked professionally and became Evan's mother. With each transition in life, I felt different—changed. Rites of passage all. Yet when did I become an adult child? And the *mother* of an adult child? *And so painfully aware of it?*

I have always loved and been attracted to older people. Fond are my memories of spending time with my elders as a small child and enjoying their company immensely. I remember them sharing stories with me of their early years and reminding me to savor and enjoy *my* childhood days with my family as they would pass quickly. And they did.

I recall clearly the months that I was pregnant with Evan and swimming with the seniors at a local pool before going to work as a dental hygienist in a practice where we had a large population of retirement aged patients. Again, they repeatedly advised me to savor the time with my baby and to truly enjoy those years as a family. I dearly loved those good souls who were living from their rich and vast experiences. Those kind ladies, grand and great grandmothers, knit Evan every conceivable garment and cozy blanket possible. It was knit-o-rama and we were the fortunate recipients. Nothing in life is a more permanent and wonderful transition than becoming a parent. We were forever blessed and though I was thirty four years old, it took motherhood for me to finally feel as if I had become a woman. There is nothing rational about that at all---simply a matter of the heart.

And I *did* savor those years---I retired from my practice to devote myself full time to my family, but it passed as quickly as they promised it would. My little old-fashioned sailor boy had become a young man, preparing to leave the nest.

And suddenly, it seemed, that the silver haired folks who were advising me this time were my contemporaries, and they were telling me from their own experience to savor the time that I had left with my own mother and father. Many of them were dealing with health issues and the death of one or both of their parents. Oh, my.

So there I was, my arms around Chasta's soft neck, sobbing into her golden hair as she patiently curled her head down to meet mine on the day Evan drove off into his future and my mother was not able to walk with her own strength. Gary and I cried together until there were no more tears. Evan had been painfully aware that his farewell to his grandmother may have been his final good-bye.

Thankfully, Evan was able to fly home to our empty nest and put his arms around Grand-ma one more time and help his mother through her most difficult transition to date: the death of a parent. I was with my mother when she took her final breath. It was both a sacred privilege and a haunting and heart-breaking moment.

Exactly twenty four hours later, my dear friend Amelia, the young woman who brought our first horse, Chad, into our lives, came to pick me up to take me to a read-ing for my newly released book in Seattle. She had been like a daughter to me in the years since the day we met and now it was her turn to *really* nurture me. In spite of the circumstances and partly because of them, it was a very powerful evening of truly honest discussions about life, mothers and horses. I felt my Mother's presence deeply and it was a great comfort. Learning and growing with horses has truly contributed to the fact that I had the emotional ability to be there at such a difficult time and have something to share in a calm, confident and peaceful way. Then Amelia returned the day of my Mother's memorial service, and sat next to me with Gary and Evan, holding my hand. And I realized that I had a son *and* a daughter. After the tribute, she left to celebrate her own Mother's birthday. And I will *never forget* how all of us joined hearts the day Chad, the horse who had brought us together, died peacefully.

My time with Chasta helped me beyond measure to fully embody this blessed yet difficult and painful experience. Walking to visit my parents allowed me to go through our pastures and connect with the horses coming and going every day. It grounded me yet I was lifted up to the clouds. It anchored my spirit and set it free. Philosopher Henry David Thoreau reminds us that: *"Heaven is under our feet as well as over our heads."* My horses have taught me the truth of those words.

About a week before she made her transition, the woman who once gave me life had now lost her vigor and strength to become skeletally thin and pale and was lying beside me as I read her to sleep. Communication was only possible for short periods each day and I could feel the heaviness in my own eyelids and heart. *"Mom,"* I started, leaning toward her. "I know that you have been living between the worlds and seeing what you call "shining angels" and I believe that when you do make your transition that you will come to me and it will be apparent, but I wonder, before you fall asleep tonight, could you give me a sign on this side so that I will know *for sure?"*

Without hesitation, she opened the eye closest to me and whispered, *"I will be the wind in your hair."* Wow. I smiled weakly and the lump in my throat dissolved into bittersweet joy. *"Great,* Mom! I *love* the wind in my hair! And I also really love it when the wind ruffles my horses' manes." Her eye opened again long enough for me to barely hear her offer, *"I'll ruffle theirs, too."*

Many times since that day my horses and I have stood together and thoughts of my mother make me aware of a breeze surrounding us on an unusually still day. Or a sudden gust of wind makes me aware of my mother. God is there. And my horses' manes?

She ruffles theirs, too.

Wind Ruffled Chasta

Chapter Twenty Four

To Sleep, Perchance to Dream

Blessed with an abundance of energy and a sensitive spirit, I have always had the good fortune to be fascinated by life in general. Yet at the same time, this big and buzzing energy has often been associated with a *far too busy* mind. I can still recall distinctly the thought form when in my twenties, that sleep was actually *such* a waste of my time! If only I had those sleeping hours, just think of all of the things that could be *done,* was a crazy thought circulating in my overactive left brain.

And that's it. I was modeled and groomed by society and my family system to be a human *do*ing rather than a human *be*ing. My value as a person seemed intimately linked to what I accomplished rather than the essence of who I was as a soul. We need to understand *both* as invaluable.

Now that I am experiencing the often disrupted sleep patterns of a menopausal woman, I can hardly believe that youthful naivete ever existed! Sleep is restoration and regeneration just as food is nourishment and fuel. And, oh, how I crave every glorious moment of restful sleep!

You may have seen the fascinating film about the story of Dr. Jill Bolte Taylor called *My Stroke of Insight.* She also published a book of the same title, which is a more detailed and *incredible* account of her journey of brain trauma and recovery. Before her stroke, Dr. Bolte Taylor was already remarkably balanced in both hemispheres of her brain as an intellectual left brained scientist as well as a gifted right brained musician and artist.

Yet her stroke and recovery offered her an opportunity to realize many amazing insights into the human mind and how much we can engage on a conscious level to communicate with our brain and other organs, our emotions and feelings to make *deliberate choices* for health and well being. She found healing in the *Feldenkrais* method for whole brain integration and made the choice for restorative sleep as *paramount* to her recovery. Her book is a brilliant and valuable resource to *everyone*.

My Mother was the ultimate human *do*ing. She was *incredibly* generous in spirit and continually gave of herself to others. To the point of her own peril.

I fully realize that service to others is what makes life worthwhile and gives us meaning and purpose, and yet Mom did almost nothing to rest and renew her own energy until her physical functions declined rapidly at a far too early age.

It was fascinating in the last few years and months she was alive that Mom began to have a rich dream life, often in the form of disturbing nightmares, as she tried to sort out and understand her disabilities. She could no longer be the servant she had been so faithfully throughout her life, and depending on and receiving help was foreign to her.

Though I am not an expert in Jungian psychology, Mom and I had some very special moments while I took dictation from her of the remarkable details of her dreams and then looked up the symbols of various archetypes together. Her recall was so vivid, even when she could barely talk and her focus incredible. Some of the dream symbols seemed so obscure and unrelated that I felt they were undecipherable, and yet each one had rich meaning and created a very healing story of accepting, understanding and letting go. *Even rejoicing*. It gave Mother and Daughter tremendous relief and insights. My own dreams were rich and vivid, too, as I tried to sort out my new role as caregiver and grieving adult child.

Because my Mother was a product of a pioneering work ethic, a family that valued service, and robbed of a great deal of her childhood innocence by the death of her father at an early age, she was only comfortable when giving herself away. *Service and hard work are wonderful and very important attributes*, yet if valued in the extreme can create dysfunction. Sonia Choquette cites a Chinese proverb in her inspiring book, *Your Heart's Desire: "When you are willing to receive what you are willing to give and when you are willing to give what you are willing to receive, then you understand love."* This is a challenging lesson, but certainly rings true.

Horses are keenly aware of their need for deep sleep to remain healthy, yet equine DNA dictates that the only way it is safe to let go and sleep lying down to get to the restorative levels is when another herd member acts as guard and sentry in awareness of potential predators. This is true even in domesticity. I believe that the early decline in health of our Arabian horse, Ritzy, was in large part to his ongoing lack of the deepest levels of restful sleep. He did not allow himself the luxury of lying down and apparently felt his role as caregiver for Chasta was more important than his own health. Much like my Mother. My Mother was a quiet and humble disciple of Christ by *living* his teachings. She embodied the words of The Dalai Lama when he said "Kindness is my religion." I simply wish that she had treated *herself* just a little more kindly. Rested more. Eaten some of the fancy chocolate that I brought her rather than always saving it for company. Occasionally taken a lingering bubble bath rather than a thirty second shower.

Today I continue to seek balance with an active life of pursuing personal interests and health as well as continued service to others. I live in the grateful awareness of my left brain that is able to do, do and do some more, but also absolutely *cherish* the quiet mind of my right hemisphere and know that restful sleep restores both.

In the wonderful words of Dr. Jill Bolte Taylor, "*My stroke of insight is: peace is only a thought away, and all we have to do to access it is silence the voice of our dominant left mind."*

On that note, it is time for me to get out my dream journal, lay still and enjoy the waking dreamtime of meditation. And with any luck, I will fall fast asleep.

Bitaritz, affectionately known as *Ritzy.*

Deep Sleep at the Gateway 2 Ranch
Courtesy Liz Mitten Ryan

Chapter Twenty Five

Perspective

Weather forecasters predicted the snow-storm accurately. It was the most extended freeze with ongoing snow flurries in over fifty years here in the Pacific Northwest. Since living on the coast usually means fairly mild winters with infrequent light snow, the locals are always caught off guard and unprepared when a big storm hits. The stores sold their entire inventories of snow shovels and antifreeze and even airports cancelled hundreds of flights because they ran out of de-icer for the runways. The highways were in gridlock with vehicles strewn in ditches in every direction. So basically, the wintry days were interrupted by chaos.

And yet for me, having two feet of snow (when we are used to having mere inches) gave me a pleasant reprieve from a too busy schedule the week before Christmas. In order to keep an important appointment on the second day of the storm, I ventured out and slipped and slid all over the unplowed, un-sanded icy country roads. Happy to get my business done, I came home and parked my car for the duration, grateful to accept that other holiday plans would need to be rescheduled.

Being home gave me the opportunity to spend extra time with the animals, both wild and domestic, helping them to stay warm, dry and well fed. Chasta and Gaela looked like pretty Christmas ornaments wrapped in their colorful winter blankets against the bright white background that surrounded them. It gave me pause to savor the incredible beauty of the twinkling snow blanket that covered the farm fields as far as my eyes could see and the barns and country homes that dot the rural landscape here. I loved watching Evan's new and adorable black Labrador puppy, Cooper, cavort in the deep snow as he got to know his skeptical and jealous older dog brothers as the three of them marked territory and created yellow snow. It was a true blessing to live close enough to my father to be able to walk down and prepare him a hot meal when he was similarly homebound the first Christmas season after he was without his wife of nearly fifty six years—my mother.

Walking home after a visit, the deep snow over the top of my highest boots, I thought of how much I missed my Mom and the lyrics of her favorite Christmas Carol, *Good King Wenceslas,* whispered softly in my ears. It was her voice that I heard singing, the one I had listened to many times before:

"In his master's steps he trod, where the snow lay dinted, Heat was in the very sod, which the Saint had printed. Therefore gentle folk, be sure, wealth or rank possessing, Ye who now will bless the poor, shall yourselves find blessing."

A wave of bittersweet joy rushed through me and my steps felt lighter as I recalled the Christmas season when Evan had his first cello lesson. On his own, he approached us with the desire to learn to play and I could not find a teacher fast enough. Yet it proved to be a series of telephone calls based on referrals which led to answering machines and the days turned into a few weeks. Finally I was given the name of a woman who came highly recommended who lived on nearby Whidbey Island. Startled to hear a real voice on the other end of the line on the first ring, I introduced myself and told her that my son, Evan, would love to learn to play the cello and wondered if we could set up a time. "How about tomorrow at 4 pm?" was the cheerful reply. *"Oh, my!* That would be wonderful!" I said with surprised delight.

The next day I eagerly packed a snack and Evan's new rental cello and picked him up after school on the last day of November to head for his lesson and meet his new teacher. As excited as his mother, Evan said clearly and triumphantly, *"I am going to learn to play Good King Wenceslas for Grandma this Christmas!"* His words touched me deeply and were so innocent and sincere that I did not want to burst his bubble, so I chose mine carefully: "Oh, *honey!* That is such a great idea! But it will probably take a while to learn something this new to you, so it may be simple scales this season and *next* Christmas you can play it for her!" My words did not change the quiet smile on the face of my little boy, my old soul, as he crunched on the apple I brought for him.

We arrived as Marjorie McNae was finishing with another student and I loved everything about her immediately. Warm, gracious, relaxed and engaging, she was *exactly* what I had envisioned as a music teacher. My plan was to quietly observe the lessons and learn all I could since my interest in music was as keen as Evan's though neither of us had ever played a stringed instrument.

Evan was quietly focused and they developed an instant rapport. Within a half an hour, I was intent, but somewhat lost and confused, as they were happily learning bow position and fingerings together. The minutes ticked away and I felt like an old dog having trouble learning new tricks as I looked at my watch and realized that there were only a few minutes left.

Mrs. McNae suddenly announced in a breezy voice, *"Well, Evan, you are ready to play your very first melody!* She flipped through the pages thoughtfully and finally said, "Here's a lovely song, just in time for Christmas--- *Good King Wenceslas.*"

Within six feet of the two of them and their beautifully curved instruments, I was glad to be sitting down because I could feel my body fall back against the chair as my jaw dropped. Evan had never stated his intention out loud, as I had been there the entire time! When he turned to beam at me, he did not look incredulous, only confident, as if he knew it all along. In the next moment, the skilled hand of a symphony level cellist who bows a burled hardwood instrument from the 1700's led a small child on his shiny new half sized model from the music store as they played my Mother's beloved carol that had become our favorite as well. And indeed, Evan played it for his Grandmother Kay not only that Christmas, but that *very* night! *Incredible!* Oh ye, *(Me!)* of little faith!

The next day, I saw a small brass Christmas ornament in the shape of a music stand. I purchased three of them. One for Mrs. Mc Nae, one for Evan and one for my Mother. Then I took the sheet music for *Good King Wenceslas*, reduced it down on the copy machine to a two inch rectangle and glued one to each of the miniature stands. And a few Christmases later, Evan and Marj played *Good King Wenceslas* in perfect two part harmony at a benefit concert for *Habitat for Humanity* and again with his youth symphony, both times with my Mother sitting next to me, each of us beaming through tears in the audience.

On the first Christmas since my Mother's death, the little brass music stand ornament remains a treasure, and this year it was Evan's girlfriend, Devyn, who hung it on our tree, sweetly symbolizing young love and new beginnings.

Continuing to trudge up the hill slowly in the deep snow savoring the memories, I looked up to see a very unusual perspective of our home atop the hill on Pleasant Ridge. The huge evergreen trees that frame the back of our house were flocked in the heavy snow so beautifully that the vision took my wintry breath away. Each one was distinct from the next, outlined in their crystal white perfection. Sometimes we do not see the forest for the trees, but this was in reverse. This time I realized that since the surrounding evergreens are so ubiquitous here as to seem commonplace, they looked so different since now I could clearly see how tall and grand each one was individually and appreciate their scale and beauty in a completely new way. Feeling as if I have always been deeply connected to the old trees that grace our property, especially since losing a number of them in storms over the years, I vowed to appreciate them even more as I stared, literally, at their grandeur from this vantage point in the middle of the snow covered road as they loomed in the distance.

And in that moment, I realized that my perspective as a mother and an adult child was forever changed by the death of my own mother. As one of my friends whose mother had died a few years previously said when she heard our sad news—"Now you are a member of a club that you did not choose to join." It was true. And yet, my experience can provide me with a new level of understanding and compassion for others. As my grieving heart heals, I can be a comfort to those who are experiencing their own pain and loss as the health of a parent declines and leads to death.

Those snowy two weeks when I was mostly home close to my human and animal family gave me special time to feel deeply. Sometimes the sadness felt as if it might crowd out all else. On Christmas night, Evan built a fire outside by the Scarlet Oak tree we had planted to honor Mom and had decorated for the wildlife with seeds and nuts, a gift from our dear friends, John and Kathy Yaeger. We burned the dried flowers that had been so pretty at her memorial service as well as sage and sweet grass Evan and I brought from Little Big Horn. How timely that we should have provided for the wild birds and critters when their usual buffet was under drifts of snow. I thought of the previous Christmas when I had surprised my Mother with an old *Lassie* movie from her childhood starring Elizabeth Taylor and Roddy McDowell. Mom was all propped in pillows since she did not have the strength to sit up on her own and remembered the film as if not separated by the years. She began to cry when Lassie was returning to her family the five hundred miles from Edinborough and had crossed a raging river and limped along the shore. Her eyes were wide and filled with tears when she whispered, "Her paws are bloody" and sure enough, *in the next frame*, the camera panned down to her bleeding feet. How the memory stores deep emotion! How careful we must be that what is there is tended to in awareness. Standing there by the fire leaning on my husband and son, I cried until the tears came no more.

And how fascinating my perspective a week later when it thawed and rained enough to expose the ground and the grass and dirt looked so unfamiliar! As odd and new as the thick blanket of white had a few weeks before. And that I had completely forgotten the winter Heather hedges were in their full and glorious fuchsia toned bloom, hidden and waiting silently for the thaw. I vowed to not allow them to go unappreciated since the plants from my ancestral home of the British Isles where the *Lassie* movie was filmed are such a bright spot in the winter landscape. How quickly we as pattern animals adapt to our surroundings! What creatures of habitual perception we become.

But on the other end of the spectrum of adjusting to death, I remembered with joy the birth of my niece, Callie, when a wonderful article she wrote appeared in the local paper about sustainable green practices for the holiday season. She is the recycling and composting educator for the county and nothing could have made her grandmother more proud or would have been truer to her own heart than Callie's words. After all, this was the woman who posted a sign on the cabinet next to where the toilet paper roll hung when I was a small child that read: *"Take Ye not thirty squares if three will do nicely!"*

Thinking back to my niece's arrival into the world made me remember the day my sister called to say they were at the clinic where she was to have a natural birth. The experience was a mountaintop memory like nothing else I had ever felt in my young adult life until the birth of our own child. My sister had called me at work and I thanked my staff for covering for me as I flew out the door with my bag packed. The birth classes that I had attended had prepared me on many levels, and numerous friends had given me the privilege of being an honorary auntie to their children, but nothing could compare with seeing Callie emerge as a new life into the world. When the final push revealed her body, the doctor surprised me completely when he asked, *"Well*, what is it? since my head was the closest and my eyeballs were out on stalks. I felt like an amateur, as I scanned her bluish body, trying carefully to find my perspective. What had seemed like an amorphous blob a few seconds before, suddenly limbs literally popped open and I finally felt I could make the call---"She's a *girl!*" I hollered as I felt myself jump for joy and heard her proud grandparents cheering through the doorway. My sister looked tired but *supremely* beautiful and radiant as she cut the umbilical cord of her daughter, the first grandchild in our family.

My life had changed. *Enormously.* I had witnessed the live birth of a human being! Knowing life was precious and that each one is absolutely *miraculous* took on a completely new meaning for me. Very late that evening, I saw my reflection in the mirror and recognized the little babe inside who had emerged 28 years before in a completely new light. I wanted to shout from the rooftops that life was so precious and amazing and was tempted to stop strangers on the street to ask them if they knew, *truly*, that they were a *miracle.* It seemed that if we could only legislate a way to require everyone to witness the beauty of live birth, it could change the world.

Today my lovely niece is nearly 28 herself and the circle of life continues. She and I had some very tender days and nights together shortly before the death of our mother/grandmother, dosing out her medication, trying to keep her comfortable, hoping and praying that our care was what she needed most. It was deeply intimate for me, like the day of her birth, to watch her capable hands care for my mother, the same ones that had popped into view so suddenly from her first indefinite form.

Finally, without question, my time in close companionship with horses has changed my perspective significantly forevermore. I am getting to know myself on deeper levels every day through their eyes. They are so fun and funny, resilient and wise and remind me that I am, too. Because their perspective as horses is so much different than mine, it requires me literally to attempt to walk in their shoes (although my mares are barefoot naturally!). This awareness of a point of view different than my own perspective has helped me to better look at how I experience *all life* and my place in it. First Nations Salish Chief Dan George said: *"If you talk with the animals, they will talk with you and you will know each other. If you do not talk with them, you will not know them and what you do not know, you will fear. What one fears, one destroys."*

So today as I begin a new year and write goals for my life to be the best person that I can be, I think of the perspective, the lens through which I see life. And I know that the experiences that have shaped my perspective will continue to change as I learn and grow. I would like to think that I will continue to grow and blossom as much as I age and wane.

This is a hopeful perspective offered by Antonio Porchia: "A full heart has room for everything, and an empty heart has room for nothing."

My heart is full and I am ready to make room. For everything.

"The tears streamed down, and I let them flow as freely as they would, making of them a pillow for my heart. On them it rested."

Saint Augustine
Confessions 1X 12

Mourning Doves greet me

Chapter Twenty Six

Pony Longing

Not long after my front teeth erupted as a baby, when I began to walk, I tripped over the hem of my nightgown, fell down the stairs, and knocked them out as a toddler. The adults in my family taught me to sing the popular song of the forties, *All I Want for Christmas is my Two Front Teeth*, which I belted out precociously with a serious lisp from my edentulous state and a major tongue thrust dilemma for four *long* holiday seasons.

It always created big laughs, but it made me painfully aware from a tender age to be careful what you wish for, since when my permanent teeth *finally* arrived as belatedly as my primary ones were lost prematurely, they were *enormous* and protruded like an old-fashioned cow catcher on a locomotive engine. I suppose I should have been more specific! I looked and sounded like the beaver on Walt Disney's *Lady and the Tramp* and my second grade classmates reminded me of that fact on a regular basis. And though I was parroting the song that the adults thought was so funny, I truly *did* want front teeth like all the other kids my age, but what I *really* wanted for Christmas was *a pony*. A real, live pony like the ones in Marguerite Henry's *Misty Of Chincoteague.*

The closest I got was the rides at the *Lake Serene Pony Farm* which was my favorite place on the planet. The combination of the scents of those sweaty ponies, the time softened leather tack and the thicket of the forest trails thrilled me to the point of intoxication like the story from the *Anne of Green Gables* series when the girls drink raspberry cordial quite by accident and end up shocking the neighbors. Ponies made me feel that *giddy* with delight.

It was these heightened sensory experiences in the forest that included the sound of crunching twigs and cones under the hooves of the stalwart ponies and their contented snorts mixing with my blissful sighs that still feel just as real to me in this moment as they did then. The smells, the sounds and that rich tapestry of visuals. A motley group of horse-crazy kids from the city and the suburbs getting a chance to be up close and personal with real live ponies and horses. To run your chubby fingers over the tooled patterns on the shiny leather saddles and witness the dizzying array of tack and grooming tools in the weathered shed was sheer joy for me. These memorable sensory experiences planted the seeds that life on earth is meant to be as it is in Heaven so that we understand and attempt to live the Kingdom of Heaven on earth.

And even the gustatory component was a part of the sheer magic of it all since most of the times we had the privilege of going there was to celebrate a birthday. What could be better than chocolate cupcakes with butter cream frosting eaten with fingers and licking them after the last bite in the perfect crisp weather of an autumn day while the tired ponies rested as the trail leaders removed their saddles and we gave them a final brushing?

The sum total of this sensory experience was taken over the top by the kinesthetic component: my small, young body moving in time with the sturdy, agile pony turning around trees on the trail and climbing hills was the greatest embodied spiritual awakening that I had ever experienced.

God was there. Of this, I could be sure. It was not a sermon or ever discussed out loud yet all of creation tingled through me in a way that left me assured that I *mattered*. That I *belonged*. That the lake, ponies and the trees were my *family*. They did not notice my buck teeth nor did they care. They knew the comfort and joy that I was experiencing and were glad for it, happy to be pressed into service by our mutual Creator.

The feeling is what the beloved poet Mary Oliver describes when she suggests that we *"live astonished."*

What is this yearning? This longing that calls to us from the quiet yet active center of every cell, encoded in our unique DNA? I believe that it is the connection to God where we experience unconditional love. Experiencing the power within while receiving the power surrounding us.

More of the time I am living my life with an ever expanding sense of what is possible and realizing incredible moments in time that I could not even formerly fully *imagine* yet wholly content with *what is* and not wanting for more or expecting an outcome. It is what philosopher Henry David Thoreau described as "success unexpected in the common hours."

The synchronicities of life continue to fascinate me. On our return home from Indianapolis, Evan and I stopped for the famous blueberry pancakes served by a *Cracker Barrel*™ Restaurant in Wisconsin. Evan had raved about them during his year on the road racing and convinced me that we needed to indulge ourselves. Pulling off the interstate onto an exit that would allow us to refuel our low gas tank, we pulled right into a station parking lot that was next to the restaurant we were looking for without realizing it was there! After savoring the famous offering with pure maple syrup (which *definitely* justified the calories) at a table that was next to open flames in a huge stone fireplace, we wandered through the gift shop on our way to pay our tab. The country store was filled with nostalgic Americana, and I spotted a rack that had a DVD of old episodes of *Mister Ed, The Talking Horse*, a television show from my 1950s childhood that led me to a great love of Palomino colored horses. I was *enchanted* by the adventures of Mister Ed and remember dreaming that it could happen in my life---to have a magical horse appear who would talk with me and be my special friend. I purchased the DVD for Gary's Christmas stocking and felt delighted that Evan would be able to see what we had grown up watching.

It was with an eerie sense of deja' vu that I watched the premiere episode. The unlikely premise of the show is that a young couple purchased a home in the country where a sweet older horse is left behind in a small barn by the previous renter. When they discover him, the wife has no interest (surprisingly since the attraction of women to horses is usually strong) but a wonderful childlike expression comes over the husband's face and his entire body softens as he wistfully greets and pets the horse. The humans immediately argue over keeping the animal and the wife hastily leaves to find a buyer. A silly sequence ensues when a man comes to purchase the horse and gives the wife the cash while the husband stands helplessly by and as the horse trader leads him away, Mister Ed starts walking with an exaggerated limp. The buyer pauses and asks about the lameness, as the horse hangs his head and proceeds to lie down as if he is on his last legs. The horse trader grabs his cash back and stomps off, thinking he had been set up and duped. At that moment, the horse stands up, shakes himself off and winks at the man named Wilbur who thinks he is a *wonderful* animal.

Naturally, it seems so far fetched, especially since at no time do you see the poor horse graze on a pasture or any sign of manure to muck, and yet it is the *exact real life scenario* that happened when we found our first horse, Chad. When his owner, Amelia, the love of his life, decided that she needed to sell him to be able to afford to compete with a younger horse on fifty mile endurance rides, she set out to look for the perfect family to offer him an easy going retirement. A number of people came to look him over, and every time, she said that he surveyed them warily and walked with a *pronounced limp!* Naturally, no one wanted a horse with lameness issues and Amelia was totally perplexed as to why it continued to happen. She had him evaluated by a vet and his legs x-rayed. Nothing abnormal showed up, but Chad went through the same scenario every time someone came to look. *Between times he was brand new!* Until he saw then five year old Evan run toward the fence to greet him. Chad met him half way without a trace of a limp, then looked over at me and turned to Amelia with a look that said, "OK, I *found my person!*" It was love at first sight for all of us. Amelia still shakes her head when she tells this story!

And when Mister Ed is alone with *his* new person, he is treated to a loving grooming session and Wilbur reveals his heart to him by telling this forgotten old horse that he has longed for a pony ever since he was a little boy. When the horse engages in conversation with him in reply, not only metaphorically, but *literally*, Wilbur is completely startled and asks how it is possible. Mister Ed tells him it is possible because he *likes* his new friend. That their feelings for each other are mutual. Wilbur is overwhelmed and continues to question how this exchange is happening. With the wisdom that the horse represents, Mister Ed sagely offers, "Don't try to figure it out, Wilbur. *This is bigger than both of us.*" Quite profound for 1960s TV!

As silly as this early sitcom was, it premiered in 1961, when I was six years old and at the height of my horse crazy fever. I realized even as a small child that it was within the realm of possibility that a human and a horse could have a meaningful exchange and deep bond of friendship that was *very real* and not merely a funny make-believe story. Now from an adult perspective of having experienced profound communication with horses, I watched with delight the antics of this television horse and realized it was due to many hours of training that grew out of a deep bond with humans. I felt like my inner six year old Connie was sitting on my lap watching with me! What a *wonderful full of wonder* experience! It reminded me that we all need to find that place where fairy tales meet real life and that grown men like Wilbur (and now young man Evan) need to *always* stay in touch with their pony longing. For from that longing, life continues to expand and become *bigger than all of us.*

So *Pony Longing,* I believe, is universal. Whether a person ever connects with a live four legged equine creature, the yearning is there. It manifests itself in many ways and each person's relationship with God is their unique gift.

The longing. The mystery. *The desire to go beyond the fear.* To believe in the majesty of self with equal conviction to the presence of the horse or whatever it may be that makes God visible and to humble oneself to *their* magnificence.

John O' Donohue captured this essence in his classic book of Celtic wisdom called *Anam*

Cara. He writes: *"Fashioned from the earth, we are souls in clay form. We need to remain in rhythm with our clay voice and longing. Longing is the presence of the divine."*

My prayer is that in some small way that these stories speak to *your* longing. To nourish that part of you which understands our interconnectedness. Our similarities and differences.

To hear the cries of the herd, calling us home.

Photo taken of an Irish horse gazing over the Atlantic Ocean by the niece of Father William Treacy after he celebrated at a service dedicated to the memory of John O'Donohue, author of *Anam Cara*

Epilogue

Connie Enchanted by the Carousel

The older I get, the greater is the realization that I know a lot about a few things, quite a bit about many things and very little about most things. Rather than allowing that fact to be cause for concern that time is running out and the world is moving ahead without me, I choose to embrace that being a full time student of life is my forever gift.

Becoming a horsewoman has improved my ability to stay open and curious to the process of communication and plunging into continuously unknown territory. Though we may have charted our courses carefully, the future remains largely unknown, so my goal is to frame that which I cannot control (mostly everything!) as interesting, exciting, and hopefully I can achieve the relatively constant level of *absolutely fascinating!*

As a child, sometimes the movement of spinning made me feel very dizzy and disoriented and at other times I reveled in it. It seemed to have to do with focus---on the carousel I was enchanted by my wondrously carved pony and the musical trill of the calliope or spinning with one knee and my arms locked onto the playground bars at recess in elementary school was an exciting new sensation.

So today, I use those happy feelings that are recorded in the cellular memory of my heart to return to if life seems to be spinning faster than is comfortable or the rug seems to have been pulled abruptly out from under me.

Interestingly enough, that expression originated from the practice of Asian masters pulling prayer rugs out from under their students without warning to test their ability to maintain equilibrium on every level. Certainly illness, death of a loved one, loss of economic security, accidents, children entering or leaving the nest qualify as tugging at our rugs, so how do we find and maintain our spiritual center that is at the hub of our personal wheel of life?

For me, the evolving process centers on trusting that there truly are angels assigned to support me in so many forms if I but believe and feel their presence with hope and gratitude. That God and the legions of angels are so much bigger, greater and stronger than anything that I can present as a need.

In the few weeks before my Mother's death, she was in a transition between the worlds. When she was awake, she often looked up and out the window toward the light with a faraway look in her eyes. Once in particular, she was very wide eyed and seemed concerned, even frightened. *"What is it, Mom? What do you see?"* I asked. *"Angels"* she whispered, still looking toward her vision. "Shining *angels!*"

"How many?" I queried. "Lots and lots" she returned, her face softening a bit toward the light coming in through the window. "Do they look female or male?" I continued. "Both" was her reply. I sat with her quietly for a few minutes while she was deeply in another realm.

"Are you afraid?" I finally whispered. *"No."* was her immediate answer. At this point, her eyes closed and an incredible expression of peace settled on her frail yet still remarkably beautiful features.

Leaning over to whisper, I offered *"I'm so glad the shining angels are there with you, Mom"* and kissed her on the forehead. She smiled without opening her eyes.

A week later, she was very near the end and had little interest or ability to eat or drink and was hardly able to speak above a whisper or at all. Opening her eyes suddenly she startled me by saying *clearly*, "We are having pizza, apples and carrots!" I was confused and thought she meant that the family members and caregivers surrounding her were having lunch. It really touched me since she was always thinking of others and had continuously made a point of sending me home with apples and carrots for my horses. She saved every scrap of them when chopping carrots for a hearty soup or apples for one of her incomparable pies.

So with my hand over hers, I told her that we had already eaten and then asked if *she* was hungry. *"No"* she started again, looking directly into my eyes. "We are having pizza, apples and carrots *here!*" Riveted, I asked "Who is with you?" She looked and sounded completely childlike when she answered *"Jesus and the angels."* A shudder of electric energy ran up my spine and I smiled through the tears. "You said apples and carrots, Mom. Does that mean there are *horses* with you, too?"

"Yes!" she whispered with confidence. *"Yes."*

She smiled, and closed her eyes. Mission accomplished. The message was received and delivered. Received again and now delivered again. *To you.*

"The Legend" by Kim McElroy

A Mother's Love

At the same moment my mother took her final breath, Alpaca baby Thulisa took her first as she emerged from her mother, Eve, a few miles down the road... Thulisa is the Zulu word for peace.

Photo by Ray Nichols
Eve and Thulisa are part of the Alpaca Adventures family of John and Kathy Yaeger (360) 708-1151

Acknowledgements

The most overwhelming feeling throughout this process has been one of gratitude. For the opportunity to be able to attempt to put into words what has meant so much to me that I felt led to share. So thank you, God, for giving me life to tell the tales.

This book is dedicated to my Mother, Kay, who is the primary editor. Her talent for language, grammar and the ability to create word pictures supported me until the day she died and beyond. When her body made its retreat, I felt continuously guided to cross every 't' and dot every 'i', and am never at a loss for the best possible word to convey my meaning, as it is only a deep breath and a closed eyed request away. My utmost gratitude goes to my other editors and layout professionals, Marella Dubuque, Carolyn Allyn-Stone, Kate Morgan and especially Davina Andrée. They made this book possible. And to Jeremy Townsend and Kat Mack of *PublishingWorks* who know how to create a beautiful finished product. And my biggest fan, my Father, Glen. I will always be grateful for the fact that he is *certain* that I have been called to share stories. My parents have been my most faithful audience. I am honored by my brother Craig and his wife Lisa for believing in me and sharing Craig's stunning portrait of Black Elk.

Friends truly are the flowers in our gardens and without them, life would not have its vibrant color. My heartfelt gratitude to Kim McElroy, for again sharing her incredible artwork in the form of *Spirit Sketches*™ within the text as well as *The Legend,* one of her most popular images and the beautiful *Halcyon* on the back cover. The image of *Halcyon* visits me in meditation and dreams and has been a continual source of inspiration and peace for me. I am truly thankful to Deborah Koff-Chapin, the creator of *Touch Drawing*™ for the profound cover art image from her *Soul Cards*™ series. To my friend and mentor Stormy May for her gift of the Foreword and inspiring me with her courage to seek more intimacy and honesty with ourselves and our horses. Daily I am grateful to Kathy Yaeger for her steadfast friendship that always feels like a sacred foundation for me to build on. Likewise to Sandra Wallin for continual encouragement to follow my heart and the ability to be a wise and caring guide. Always to Amelia Tritz for being my girl as we grow up together. My heart is grateful to Barbara Rector and Linda Kohanov for blazing trails that so many of us have been blessed to follow. To Liz Mitten Ryan for opening many doors for me—your generous spirit is an inspiration. To Carolyn Resnick, Pat and Linda Parelli and Jonathan Field and many other horsemen and women for continuing to raise the bar on yourselves with horses so your students can follow in your paths.

For my advanced readers—you are my admired friends—what a leg up you have been for me! Barbara Rector, E. Bailey Tune, Sandra Wallin, Linda Kohanov, Liz Mitten Ryan, Rita Reynolds, Kerri Lake, Dianna McPhail, Stormy May, Vicki Graves-Mitchell, Patricia Kelley, Kathy Yaeger, Jaye Nichols, Carolyn Allyn Stone, Kim McElroy, Robin Carneen, Lori Keehr, Mark Mottershead, Sandra Seiden, Sharon Roberts, Davina Andrée, Vicki Talbott and Leif Hallberg.

Your belief in these stories is my gift.

For all of the readers of my first book for taking your time to send me such *incredible* correspondence of how our lives and stories are connected and how we can help and support each other while listening to Nature's communications from a loving Creator. For all of my family and friends who have been a part of my life in so many wonderful and sometimes prickly ways.

And especially to Gary and Evan, for knowing what our animal family means to me and loving them like I do. For telling me that you are proud of my efforts and supporting them all along the way. For Devyn—what a blessing you are to all of us.

But mostly to the horses who have rocked my world in the most amazing ways. Chad, Ritzy, Gaela and my one and only Chasta. Many other horses have been a source of inspiration and education to me, but the four who have lived here in my ongoing care have been the greatest teachers I will ever know.

Photo by Evan Funk

There is in every true woman's heart
A spark of Heavenly fire,
Which lies dormant in the
Broad daylight of prosperity,
But kindles up and beams and blazes
In the dark hours of adversity.

~ Washington Irving

About the Author

Launched into another realm at midlife by her gifthorse mare, Chasta, Connie took the opportunity for growth and change to heart and began studying natural horsemanship and equine guided development in earnest. Thus began her desire to share her journey with others in her first book, **Beauty From Brokenness**, *Bits and Pieces Of My Journey Into Wholeness*.

Today, she has taken the sum total of what she is passionate about in life and made it her business and pleasure. She teaches children on a volunteer basis about gardening, composting, recycling and compassionate animal care and communication, learning as much herself from the children and animals. Woodylane Farm in rural Washington State is also a destination for equine guided development workshops with her friend and mentor, Sandra Wallin of Chiron's Way (www.chironsway.com) as well as facilitating Psych-K™ techniques one on one or with groups. Expressive arts are incorporated into the workshops and are also available for private sessions or group classes, mosaics being Connie's signature specialty.

She also has a line of antique ephemera reprint images collected throughout her life available on her website as well as collectibles and other antiques for sale.

Connie is available for inspirational public speaking engagements to encourage others to find the path to their hearts and follow where it leads. For more information check www.constancefunk.com   or call Connie at (360) 466-3757.

Photo by John Yeager

Recommended Resources

Information and Inspiration for Humans and Horses:

Barb Apple
www.barbapple-horseplay.net

Linda-Ann Bowling
www.unbridlinghumanpotential.com

Colleen Carr
www.naturalhorsenetwork.com

Cavalia
www.cavalia.com

Jonathan Field
www.jonathanfield.net

Leif Hallberg
The Esperanza Center
www.esperanzacenter.org

Klaus Ferdinand Hempfling
www.hempfling.com

Susanna Kellogg
www.freehorsefarm.com

Linda Kohanov
www.thetaoofequus.com

Kerri Lake
www.kerriklake.com

Stormy May
www.stormymay.com

Kim McElroy
www.spiritofhorse.com

Mark Mottershead
www.horseconscious.com

Adiva Murphy
www.adivamurphy.com

Alexander Nezorav
www.hauteecole.ru

Pat and Linda Parelli
www.parelli.com

Percy White Plume
Spirit Horse Society
Sung Nagi Okolakiciye
PO Box 430, Manderson, SD 57756
(605) 867-5834

Mark Rashid
www.markrashid.com

Barbara Rector
www.adventuresinawareness.net

Carolyn Resnick
www.dancewithhorses.com

Bonnitta Roy
www.alderlore.org

Liz Mitten Ryan
www.onewiththeherd.com

Sandra Seiden
www.personalponies.org

Alice Trindle
www.tnthorsemanship.com

Anna Twinney
www.reachouttohorses.com

Sandra Wallin
www.chironsway.com

Sonja Wingard
www.animalsasnaturaltherapy.com

Evan and Sandy in the 4th of July Parade

Favorite Books

Anam Cara By John O' Donohue

A New Earth: Awakening to Your Life's Purpose by Eckhart Tolle

Beginnings By Father Patrick Twohy

Black Beauty By Anna Sewell

Blessing the Bridge By Rita Reynolds

Cell Level Healing: The Bridge From Soul to Cell by Joyce Whiteley Hawkes, PhD.

Drawing Out Your Soul By Deborah Koff-Chapin

Everything Must Change: Jesus, Global Crises, and a Revolution of Hope By Brian McLaren

Finding Your Own North Star by Martha Beck

Healing Horses Their Way! By Marijke Van de Water

He Is My Brother by Father William Treacy

Honey: A Pony's Tale by Sharon Roberts

Horton Hatches The Egg By Dr. Seuss

Keep the Faith, Change the Church by James Muller & Charles Kenney

Molly The Pony, By Pam Kaster

My Callie Girl by Kimbra Kern

My Stroke of Insight by Dr. Jill Bolte Taylor

Naked Liberty by Carolyn Resnick

Non-Violent Communication: A Language of Life by Marshall Rosenberg, PhD.

On the Right Lead by Dianna McPhail

Radical Acceptance: Living Life With the Art of a Buddha by Tara Brach, PhD.

Saint Francis of Assisi : A Life Of Joy by Robert F. Kennedy, Jr.

The Field by Lynn McTaggart

The Horse Boy by Rupert Isaacson

The Soul of a Horse by Joe Camp

The Story of My Life By Helen Keller, with Annie Sullivan and John Albert May

The Truth According To Horses By Liz Mitten Ryan

Three Cups of Tea by Greg Mortenson and David Oliver Relin

Tuning In: Equine Cranio-Sacral Therapy and Somato-Emotional Release by E. Bailey Tune, LMT, CST

Walking the Way of the Horse: Exploring the Power of the Horse Human Relationship by Leif Hallberg

Go to: www.horsebooksandponystories.com for more titles from Sharon's Corner Bookstore

Film and Audio Books:

The Path of the Horse

A Documentary Film by Stormy May

Over The Hills and Far Away
A Film by Michel Orion Scott and Rupert Isaacson

Our Spirits Don't Speak English
Available from the SW Indian Foundation

Roots by Alex Hailey
Book and Film Series

Spontaneous Evolution by Dr. Bruce Lipton and Steve Bhaerman
Book and CD Series

Wild At Heart: The Radical Teachings of the Christian Mystics
by Tessa Bielecki
CD Series

Equine Healing and Wellness:

Dianna Mc Phail
Equine Bowenwork
www.mind-bodyintuition.com

Marie Pruden
Barefoot Naturally
(803) 230-8330
www.hoofarmor.net

Dr. Allen Schoen
Holistic Veterinarian
www.drschoen.com

Robyn Tatum
(250) 515-2561
http://reikiloveo.tripod.com
equinereiki@live.com

Debra Theisen
Energy Healing
(360) 778-1227

Leta Titus
Equine Herbalist/Homeopathy
(206) 384-5697

Marijke Van De Water
Equine Nutrition and Natural Remedies
www.rivasremedies.com

Equine Farm Management:

Non-Electric Waterer
Bar-Bar-A
www.horsedrinker.com

Portable Manure Spreader
Newer Spreader™
www.newerspreader.com

Personal Ponies Ltd. Celebrates Veterans' Day

Photos courtesy of Sandra Seiden, Florida State Director

May the road rise up to meet you and the wind be at your back...

Index

Symbols

A

B